10-Minute Devotions, Volume III

D1113898

Group®
Loveland, Colorado

10-Minute Devotions, Volume III
Copyright © 1993 Group Publishing, Inc.

Credits
Edited by Mike Nappa
Interior designed by Judy Bienick
Cover designed and illustrated by Liz Howe and DeWain Stoll
Contributors: Dennis Castle, Karen Dockrey, Lois Keffer, Martin Nagy, Mike and Amy Nappa, Wes Olds, Kent Place, Rex Stepp, Christy Stewart, and Steve and Annie Wamberg

Library of Congress Cataloging-in-Publication Data
10-minute devotions, volume III.
     p. cm.
    ISBN 1-55945-171-8
    1. Teenagers—Prayer-books and devotions—English.
I. Title: Ten minute devotions, volume three.
BV4850.A15 1993
242'.63—dc20   93-7811
                                                        CIP

12 11 10 9 8 7 6 5 4 3   04 03 02 01 00 99 98 97 96 95

Printed in the United States of America.

Contents

10-Minute Devotions on Christ-Centered Relationships

10-Minute Devotions on Faith Issues

10-Minute Devotions for Special Occasions

Introduction

We gave you *10-Minute Devotions for Youth Groups,* and you said, "More!"

We gave you *More 10-Minute Devotions for Youth Groups,* and you said, "It's not enough! I still need more quick devotions that help my teenagers understand and apply God's Word."

So we said, "Let's put together a fresh, new batch of fast and easy ideas to spice up Bible studies, wrap up meetings, or add deeper meaning to any activity with teenagers. Let's design each devotion to be ready in minutes—whenever a youth worker wants to grab kids' attention for a special lesson ... or cap his or her time with an experience teenagers will remember. And let's have youth leaders write it themselves, so we'll know the ideas will work."

And so, we searched high and low for the best new ideas yet—and compiled them here in *10-Minute Devotions, Volume III.* So what are you waiting for? Enjoy!

DEVOTION ELEMENTS

Each devotion consists of the following seven elements:

■ **Theme**—This is the topic of the devotion, the main thought. Themes cover a variety of teenagers' needs and concerns.

■ **Scripture**—Each devotion is based on Scripture that supports the theme and shows kids that God is concerned about every area of their lives.

■ **Overview**—This brief statement describes the devotion and tells what the participants will learn.

■ **Preparation**—This part describes exactly what materials you'll need for the devotion and what you'll need to do to prepare for it.

When preparing for the devotions, remember to involve the young people themselves. They can help round up supplies, but they can also help lead. The devotions are easy to follow and easy to prepare. Even busy teenagers can find time to prepare and lead these quick devotions. Involving teenagers as much as possible gives them ownership of the devotion and helps them develop leadership skills they will keep their whole lives.

■ **Experience**—Each devotion contains a unique element that lets kids actually experience the theme. Kids use their senses of sight, hearing, smell, touch, and taste to gain a deeper understanding of the topic being discussed.

All activities can be adapted to fit the size of your group. If you have a small group, simply do the devotional activities together. If you have a larger group, divide into small groups using a variety of methods. For example, you can divide into small groups by birth season, by color of clothing, or by shoe style. Or you can spell the theme for the devotion. If the theme is love, have the group members sound off by spelling "love." All "l's" form one group, all "o's" form another group, and so on.

■ **Response**—Participants take the experience one step further by thinking about what they've experienced and how it applies to their lives. They think about and discuss their discoveries.

■ **Closing**—Each devotion concludes with an activity that summarizes the devotional thought and helps kids apply it to their lives.

THE FOUR SECTIONS

The devotions in this book are divided into four sections for easy reference.

● **10-Minute Devotions on Personal Spiritual Growth**—Some of the themes in this section are breaking bad habits, decision making, pride, loneliness, spiritual gifts, and purity.

● **10-Minute Devotions on Christ-Centered Relationships**—Themes in this section range from friendships and family relationships to relationships with the world. Your kids will discuss topics such as competition, fun, global compassion, teachers, dating, and racism.

● **10-Minute Devotions on Faith Issues**—Your group will explore themes such as mercy, disappointment, hypocrisy, poverty, confusion, and prayer.

● **10-Minute Devotions for Special Occasions**—These devotions will put new meaning into special times like Christmas, a new school year, Passover, Easter, and graduation.

Be sure to look through the themes in this section. Some of the devotions can be used throughout the year as well as on special occasions. For example, "Seeing the Person in the Parent," on page 102, can be used for Mother's Day, Father's Day, or any time during the year when you want to stress the importance of relating well with parents.

Feel free to be creative with *10-Minute Devotions, Volume III.* Go ahead and adapt any of the quick devotions to fit a particular situation or need. And reach for this book any time, anywhere—to share fun, meaningful times that lead your kids into deeper walks with God.

10-Minute Devotions on Personal Spiritual Growth

Lemonade Imperfections

- **Theme:** Purity
- **Scripture:** Romans 12:1-2; Ephesians 5:1-3
- **Overview:** Group members will compare salty lemonade to an impure lifestyle.
- **Preparation:** Using water and lemonade mix, make enough lemonade for everyone in your group. Then add approximately one tablespoon of salt per quart of lemonade. You'll also need cups for everyone, three containers of fresh water, and Bibles.

EXPERIENCE

Form three teams and have each team select one person to be its "server." Have servers distribute cups of lemonade to their teammates. Tell kids this is a race to see which team can drink all its lemonade the fastest. On the count of three, have kids down their lemonade and see which team (if any!) finishes first.

RESPONSE

Afterward, have kids guess what was wrong with the lemonade. If no one guesses, reveal that the lemonade was made with one impure ingredient: salt. Then ask: *What did you think when you drank the lemonade? How did one impure ingredient affect the lemonade? What "impure ingredients" leave a "bad taste" in your spiritual life? in your relationships? in your thought life? in your physical well-being?*

Have kids join with members of other teams to form trios. Have trios read Romans 12:1-2 and Ephesians 5:1-3 and discuss these questions. Ask: *Why is it important for Christians to strive for purity in every area of life? In what ways are Christians tempted to sacrifice purity? What are results of striving for purity in our personal lives?*

Lemonade Imperfections

CLOSING

Have servers pour fresh water for their teammates. Say: *Just as fresh water can wash away the bad taste of salty lemonade, God can help us wash away the bad taste of impure living. Let's drink to that now.*

Have kids hold up their cups of water as you pray: *Lord, help our lifestyles be pure like water instead of impure like salty lemonade. Amen.*

On "amen," have kids drink their water to close.

Gift Giving

- **Theme:** Spiritual gifts
- **Scripture:** Romans 12:3-8; Ephesians 4:11-12
- **Overview:** Group members will examine the importance of spiritual gifts.
- **Preparation:** You'll need Bibles.

EXPERIENCE

Say: *Today is Gift Giving Day, so take a few seconds to think of a small token you can give to someone else in the group. For example, you might give a button, a penny, or a shoestring.*

Have kids form pairs and spend 30 seconds giving gifts to their partners. Then have pairs discuss these questions. Have pairs report their answers to the group after discussing each question. Ask: *How did you feel when you gave or received a gift? What would've made this a more exciting experience for you? What will you do with the gift you've received?*

RESPONSE

Have pairs read Romans 12:3-8 and Ephesians 4:11-12 and discuss these questions. Ask: *How do God's gifts compare to our gifts? Why did God give everyone different gifts? What's one spiritual gift God's given you? What's one gift from God you've noticed in your partner? What do you think God wants you to do with the gifts he's given you?*

CLOSING

Form a circle. Have kids take turns showing the gifts they received for Gift Giving Day and telling how it can remind them to use their spiritual gifts for God and others. For example, a button could remind a person to "unbutton" his or her lips and tell others about God. Encourage kids to take their gifts home as a reminder of what they learned today.

My Way or No Way

- **Theme:** Pride
- **Scripture:** Philippians 2:3-11
- **Overview:** Kids will discover the difference between pride and humility.
- **Preparation:** You'll need doughnuts for everyone and Bibles.

EXPERIENCE

Have kids form a human train by lining up behind you and holding the shoulders of the person in front of them.

Say: *I'm going to lead you on a journey around the church grounds and back to this room. During the journey, everyone must stay in the train formation and follow me. If we make it back here in three minutes or less, we'll have doughnuts for a reward. Ready? Let's go.*

Lead kids out the door and onto the church grounds. As you journey, ask kids to point out the best routes to follow, but ignore their suggestions. Instead, deliberately wander off course and waste time. For example, you might lead kids into the parking lot and through a maze of cars, or stop to smell some flowers. When kids protest, just say: *I'm the leader. I know where I'm going.*

When three minutes are up, lead kids back to the room and say: *Too bad. We didn't make it back in time to get doughnuts. But that's OK. I'll just take them home and eat them myself.*

RESPONSE

Gather the group together and have a volunteer read Philippians 2:3-11. Ask: *How did you feel during this activity? Explain. How did my attitude as your leader compare to Jesus' attitude described in Philippians 2:3-11? How would your life be different if Jesus acted pridefully like I did? How would your life be different if you acted as humbly as Jesus did?*

My Way or No Way

CLOSING

Say: *Let's practice imitating Jesus' attitude of humble service instead of my prideful attitude.*

Bring out the doughnuts and have kids take turns serving each other the sweet treats.

Two Great Tastes in One

- **Theme:** Falling short in spiritual life
- **Scripture:** Matthew 26:31-35; 69-75; John 21:15-19
- **Overview:** Kids will compare the goal of removing chocolate from a peanut butter cup to the goal of living out their beliefs.
- **Preparation:** You'll need two chocolate-coated peanut butter cups for each person, napkins, and Bibles.

EXPERIENCE

Give each group member one chocolate-coated peanut butter cup and a napkin. Challenge kids to remove and eat all the chocolate without eating the peanut butter. Give kids 30 seconds to complete the goal. Have kids who succeed share with the group their techniques for reaching the goal.

Ask: *How did you feel as you tried to remove the chocolate? Explain. What made removing the chocolate easy or difficult for you? How can hearing others' techniques help you do better in the future at removing chocolate from a peanut butter cup?*

RESPONSE

Form groups of no more than four. Have groups read Matthew 26:31-35; 69-75, then discuss the questions below. Have the oldest person in each group share answers to the first question, next oldest share answers to the second question, and so on.

Say: *Our goal was to remove chocolate from a peanut butter cup.*

Ask: *What was Peter's goal? How would you have responded in Peter's situation? How do you respond when you fall short of the goals found in the Bible? What makes it hard for you to live out your beliefs? What "techniques" can we share to help each other avoid falling short in our spiritual lives?*

Two Great Tastes in One

CLOSING

Read aloud John 21:15-19 to reassure kids with the news that even though Peter failed, Jesus didn't give up on him. And Jesus won't give up on them either.

Give each group member another peanut butter cup as a reminder to never give up on the goal of living out what they believe.

Playing by the Rules

〰〰〰〰〰〰〰〰〰〰〰〰〰

- **Theme:** Following God
- **Scripture:** 2 Peter 1:3-9
- **Overview:** Group members will examine how following God's "pattern" for life can affect the way they live.
- **Preparation:** You'll need a pair of scissors, photocopies of one page of a sewing pattern, and Bibles.

EXPERIENCE

Engage the group in a scissor-passing game called Crossed/Uncrossed. To play, have kids place their chairs in a circle and give one person a pair of scissors.

Have the first person pass the scissors to the person on his or her left. Have kids vote to see who thinks it was a "crossed" or "uncrossed" pass. Then reveal which was correct, according to the secret rule described below, and repeat the process. Tell kids they're to guess the pattern that determines whether a pass is crossed or uncrossed. Play for several rounds or until everyone catches on to the pattern. Remind kids to keep quiet when they think they know the pattern.

Here's the secret rule: What actually counts is the crossed or uncrossed position of the passer's legs. If a passer has his or her legs crossed while passing the scissors, it's a crossed pass and vice versa. If kids seem to be having trouble discovering the secret rule, clue in a person and have him or her pass the scissors with exaggerated motions to reveal the secret.

RESPONSE

Ask: *How did you feel when you discovered the pattern for the game? How did knowing or not knowing the pattern affect how you played the game? What do you think is God's "pattern" for life?*

Have kids find a partner and read 2 Peter 1:3-9. Then have pairs discuss these questions and take turns reporting their answers to the group. Ask: *What can we learn about God's "pattern" for living from this passage? How can following God's pattern affect the way you live? What makes it hard for you to follow*

Playing by the Rules

God's pattern described in 2 Peter 1:3-9? What can you do this week to overcome those obstacles?

CLOSING

Give a photocopy of one page of a sewing pattern to each person. Have kids tear out the shape on their copies as you pray a prayer like this:

Lord, help us tear away the things that prevent us from following your pattern for life. Give us strength to follow you and live according to the advice in 2 Peter 1:3-9. Amen.

Have kids take their patterns home as a reminder of the devotion.

Finders Keepers

■ **Theme:** Responsibility
■ **Scripture:** Luke 19:11-27
■ **Overview:** Group members will examine their responsibilities as Christians.
■ **Preparation:** You'll need a snack reward and Bibles.

EXPERIENCE

Form teams of no more than four and have team members number off from one to four. Then have teams select spots in the room to be their home bases and tell them to stand in those spots.

Say: *For this game, each member of your team is responsible for finding a particular item and bringing it back to your home base. The first team to have all its members back on home base with their assigned items will receive a snack reward.*

Ones, you're responsible for bringing back something you'd find in an office. Twos, you're responsible for bringing back something unusual from the parking lot. Threes, you're responsible for bringing back something red. Fours, you're responsible for bringing back something from nature. There's a three-minute time limit, so everyone be back after three minutes whether you have your items or not. Ready? Go.

RESPONSE

After everyone returns, award the snacks to the winning team Then say: *Discuss the next few questions in your teams. Then I'll call out a number from one to four. The person in your team whose number I call out will be responsible for sharing your answer.*

Ask: *How did you feel during this game? Explain. What helped you fulfill your responsibilities to your team? What made it difficult to fulfill your responsibilities? How did you overcome those difficulties?*

Have someone wearing green in each group read Luke 19:11-27. Then have groups discuss the following questions and take turns reporting their answers to the large group.

Finders Keepers

Ask: *What responsibilities does a Christian have? How are those responsibilities similar to the ones you had during the game? What attitude about responsibility does Luke 19:11-27 present? Which character in this parable is most like you? Why? What can we learn from our game to help us be more like the first or second servant in the parable?*

CLOSING

To close, have groups take turns completing this sentence: "One thing we'll do differently next week because of this devotion is..."

Oily Water

■ **Theme:** Compromising faith
■ **Scripture:** Matthew 7:24-27
■ **Overview:** Group members will see that right and wrong don't mix.
■ **Preparation:** You'll need vegetable oil, water, milk, chocolate syrup, jars with secure lids, and cups. You'll also need Bibles.

EXPERIENCE

Form two teams—team Y and team Z. Give team Y a jar of water and have team members pour vegetable oil into it. Give team Z a jar of milk and have team members add chocolate syrup to it. Tell both teams to seal their jars tightly.

Say: *Let's see which team can mix the contents of its jar most thoroughly.*

Have teams form two lines facing each other. Then have kids take turns shaking their jars for five seconds before passing the jars down their team lines. Afterward, place both jars on a table. When the oil and water separate, say to team Y: *Maybe you didn't try hard enough. Try again.*

Have team Y repeat the process. When the oil and water separate again, ask: *Why was this task easier for team Z than team Y? What feelings did you have when the oil and water didn't mix? Explain. How is trying to mix oil and water like trying to compromise Christian faith with the world's values? What are some of the world's values that don't mix with our faith?*

RESPONSE

Have teams read Matthew 7:24-27 and discuss these questions. After discussing each question, have teams select a representative to share their answers.

Ask: *How is trying to mix oil and water like building a house on sand? What tempts you to compromise God's principles in the Bible? How can you successfully "mix" your faith into your lifestyle like the way chocolate and milk mix?*

Oily Water

CLOSING

Pour everyone a drink of the chocolate milk and say: *Don't waste time trying to compromise your faith with the world's values. Instead, every time you see chocolate or milk this week, let it be a reminder for you to mix your faith into your life.*

Dismiss with a prayer asking God to help kids avoid compromising their beliefs this week. On "Amen," have kids drink their chocolate milk together as a symbol of their commitment not to compromise.

Y B Boring?

- **Theme:** Creativity
- **Scripture:** Genesis 1:1; Isaiah 42:5
- **Overview:** Kids will create a new object and explore God's creativity.
- **Preparation:** You'll need paper plates, paper clips, pencils, and Bibles.

EXPERIENCE

Give each person a paper plate, three paper clips, and a pencil.

Say: *You have three minutes to create something using only these items.*

Without giving further instructions, have group members work alone to create a new object. When time is up, have kids present and explain their creations to the group.

Ask: *How did it feel to make something with such limited resources? Were you surprised by how creative you or others were? Why is it important for people to be creative? In what ways do you like to express your creativity?*

RESPONSE

Ask two volunteers to read Genesis 1:1 and Isaiah 42:5 aloud. Have kids stand as you ask the following questions. Give them a few seconds to think after each question and tell them you'd like to hear lots of interesting responses. When one person shares an answer, anyone who thought of the same answer and has nothing more to add can sit down. When everyone is seated, ask the next question and repeat the process.

Ask: *How does God's creative work compare to ours? What in this room is evidence of God's creativity? How about in nature? What might the world be like if God refused to be creative? How can you appreciate God's creativity in life this week?*

Y B Boring?

CLOSING

Have students form huddles of no more than five members. Starting with the youngest in each huddle, have kids take turns telling each other creative qualities he or she adds to the group. For example, creative qualities might be a zany sense of humor, imaginative insight into the Bible, or musical talent.

After everyone has been affirmed, have groups join together to form one large huddle. Then close in prayer and thank God for being creative enough to make us all creative in our own ways.

Tongue Depressors

■ **Theme:** Taming the tongue
■ **Scripture:** James 3:3-12
■ **Overview:** Group members will examine how negative and unkind words "depress" speech.
■ **Preparation:** You'll need enough tongue depressors for each person to have two (most craft stores carry these), pencils, and Bibles.

EXPERIENCE

Give each person a tongue depressor and say: *Press down on your tongue with the tongue depressor. Then walk around the room and compliment as many people as you can. Remember, keep your tongue depressor firmly pressed against your tongue while giving compliments.*

After several minutes gather students together and allow them to remove the tongue depressors.

Ask: *What's it like to talk with your tongue "depressed?" Could you understand the compliments being shared with you? How did you feel while doing this activity? How is the way the tongue depressor kept you from communicating encouragement like the way negative and unkind words keep us from communicating positively with others?*

RESPONSE

Form groups of no more than four. Tell groups to read James 3:3-12 and discuss the following questions. After each question, have kids take turns sharing their group's answers. Ask: *How is your tongue like a horse's bit, a rudder, or a flame? How do you feel when you hear both good and bad words coming from the same mouth? How can God help tame your tongue?*

Have kids break their tongue depressors and throw them away as a symbol of how they're free to speak good things.

Tongue Depressors

CLOSING

Say: *Let's use our words to build others up instead of tear them down.*

Give each person a new tongue depressor. Have students write the following sentence on their depressor, completing it with a positive quality about the person to their right: "Having you here adds _____ to our group." Kids might fill in the blank with words like "friendliness," "happiness," or "kindness."

To close, have students exchange tongue depressors, reading aloud the words they've written.

Bag Heads

- **Theme:** Loneliness
- **Scripture:** Psalm 46:10-11
- **Overview:** Group members will sit silently with bags over their heads, then discuss the positive and negative aspects of loneliness.
- **Preparation:** You'll need paper bags and Bibles.

EXPERIENCE

Give everyone a paper bag, then have kids scatter around the room and sit on the floor. Say: *I want you all to sit silently for three minutes with your bags over your heads. This experience won't work unless everyone maintains perfect silence, so don't communicate with anyone in any way. I'll tell you when three minutes are up. Ready? Bag it!*

After three minutes call time and collect the paper bags. Then ask: *How did you feel during this experience? How was this experience like lonely times you've had? Explain. How easy or difficult is it for you to be by yourself? Why?*

RESPONSE

Have kids form trios and read Psalm 46:10-11 together. Then have kids share in their trios: 1) one time they felt lonely and how they responded; 2) what, if anything, they learned from that time; and 3) ways Psalm 46:10-11 could encourage them during a lonely time.

After about three minutes, call kids together and invite them to share what they discussed in their trios.

Say: *Lonely times can be painful, but they can be growing times, too. Sometimes God uses loneliness to get our attention. And we're never really alone when we're in God's presence.*

CLOSING

Have kids stand in a circle with their arms around each other's shoulders. Close with prayer, thanking God for the love and comfort of God's family.

Out of Control

■ **Theme:** Breaking bad habits
■ **Scripture:** Philippians 4:8-9
■ **Overview:** Kids will attempt to walk a straight line after spinning around, then discuss how bad habits can spin them out of control.
■ **Preparation:** You'll need masking tape and Bibles.

EXPERIENCE

Form teams of no more than four and have them each line up at one end of a masking tape line approximately 10 feet long. (You'll need one tape line for each team.) Have team members gather around the first person in their line and spin him or her around 10 times, counting the spins out loud. After 10 spins, have that person walk to the end of the tape and back without ever stepping off the tape.

Give kids who step off the tape a second chance by allowing them to go back to the beginning, spin three times, and start over. Repeat until all team members have had an opportunity to participate.

RESPONSE

When teams finish, have them sit in circles and discuss these questions: *How did it feel to try to stay on the tape when you were dizzy? What bad habits can cause people to spin out of control in real life? How can God us help break or avoid those habits?*

CLOSING

Have kids form pairs and read Philippians 4:8-9 together. Have pairs brainstorm habits that demonstrate the qualities listed in these verses. Then have group members tell their partners one bad habit they'd like to replace with a good habit. Close by having partners pray for each other.

Blind Choice

- **Theme:** Decision making
- **Scripture:** Isaiah 30:21
- **Overview:** Kids influence a volunteer to make a favorable choice, then ask for God's guidance in decision making.
- **Preparation:** Gather a large bag of M&M's, a water-filled squirt gun, and two paper bags. Keep these items hidden from group members. You'll also need Bibles.

EXPERIENCE

Choose a volunteer to leave the room. Then form two teams and designate one "Pizza" and the other "Hamburger." When the volunteer is out of earshot, show kids the squirt gun and candy.

Say: *In a moment, I'm going to cover these items with bags. Then I'll bring the volunteer back in the room and ask him* (or her) *to choose a bag. The Pizza team will get the contents of whichever bag the volunteer chooses, and the Hamburger team will get the contents of the other bag. That means if the volunteer chooses the bag with the M&M's, the Pizzas get to eat candy, and the Hamburgers get wet. If the volunteer chooses the bag with the squirt gun, the Pizzas get wet and the Hamburgers get the candy.*

You may try to influence which bag the volunteer chooses by telling him (or her) *which bag to choose, but you can't reveal what's in the bags or why you want the volunteer to pick a certain bag. You also can't move from your spot or touch the volunteer in any way.*

Place the squirt gun and candy in separate bags. Then bring the volunteer back into the room. Have him or her listen to the group members and choose a bag. Afterward, give candy and squirts to the appropriate teams.

RESPONSE

Ask the volunteer: *How did you feel making this decision? How did you decide who to listen to?*

Blind Choice

Ask the rest of the group: *How was this activity like decisions you face in everyday life? Who do you listen to when you have a decision to make?*

Have kids find a partner from the opposing team and read Isaiah 30:21 together. Have teenagers tell their partners one way God has guided their decision making in the past and one decision they're facing in the future. Then have kids brainstorm how they can hear God's "voice" directing them in future decisions.

CLOSING

Close by having pairs line up against a wall. Have one person in each pair cover his or her partner's eyes and lead the partner "blindfolded" across the room. As kids are leading, have them pray silently for their blindfolded partners, asking for God's guidance in future decisions. When everyone has reached the opposite wall, have kids switch roles and repeat the process.

I'm Wishing For...

■ **Theme:** Vanity
■ **Scripture:** Psalm 131; Psalm 139:13-14
■ **Overview:** Kids complete a wish list of outward characteristics, then discuss the fact that God made them who they are.
■ **Preparation:** Make photocopies of the "Wish List" handout (p. 35) for each person. You'll also need pencils and Bibles.

EXPERIENCE

Distribute the "Wish List" handout and say: *Use this wish list to construct the perfect you. Don't let anyone see what you write and don't sign your name. Raise your hand when you're done, and I'll collect your handout. Then we'll share what you wrote—anonymously.*

Give kids a few minutes to complete their handouts, then collect, shuffle, and read the handouts aloud to the class.

RESPONSE

Ask: *How would it feel to receive the qualities you wished for? Do you think most people are content with who they are? Explain. Do you think you'd be happier if you had a perfect body or a brilliant mind? Explain. In what ways do people pursue making themselves "perfect"?*

Form pairs and have kids read Psalm 131 and Psalm 139:13-14 with their partners. Have pairs discuss these questions and report their answers to the group. Ask: *What do these passages tell you about yourself? How do the attitudes presented in these scriptures compare to the attitudes of our wish lists? How can we bring our attitudes about outward appearances in line with the attitudes presented in these scriptures?*

CLOSING

Say: *Many of us would like to be gorgeous, talented, and wealthy. But God made us who we are for a reason. Instead of*

I'm Wishing For...

wishing for something more, we should be thanking God for who we are. Let's do that now.

To close, form a circle and have kids take turns completing this sentence prayer: "God, one thing about myself I want to thank you for is ..." Dismiss with a group hug.

Wish List

Complete the following wish list to create the "perfect" you.

I wish I could have the brains of

_____

the body of

_____

the TALENT of

_____

the fame of

_____ and

the wealth of

_____ .

10-Minute Devotions on Christ-Centered Relationships

Are We Having Fun Yet?

■ **Theme:** Fun
■ **Scripture:** Luke 15:1-10
■ **Overview:** Group members will experience a minicelebration as they explore God's perspective on fun.
■ **Preparation:** You'll need marshmallows, upbeat background music, and ice cream sandwiches for everyone. You'll also need a Bible.

EXPERIENCE

Begin class by reading aloud Luke 15:1-10 with expression. Then say: *This passage says angels celebrate when one person turns from sin to God. So let's join in the fun!*

Lead the group in a minicelebration compressed into six minutes. For the first two minutes, play a marshmallow-toss game. Give each person three marshmallows and have kids form pairs. Have partners stand 10 feet apart and toss their marshmallows in each others' mouths. See who can catch all three. Play upbeat music in the background during the game.

For the next two minutes, sing upbeat songs such as "Jesus Is the Rock" or "Shut De Do" as fast as you can. (These songs, plus many more fun songs are available in *The Group Songbook,* published by Group.)

For the final two minutes, let everyone eat ice cream sandwiches and talk while upbeat music plays in the background.

RESPONSE

Turn off the music and gather everyone in the center of the room. Have kids raise their ice cream wrappers in the air as you ask the questions below. Give kids a few seconds to think after each question and tell them you'd like to hear lots of interesting responses. When one person shares an answer, anyone who thought of the same answer and has nothing more to add can lower his or her wrapper. When all wrappers are lowered, ask the next question and repeat the process.

Ask: *How did you feel during this minicelebration? Explain. How do you think God feels about it? Explain. Why do*

Are We Having Fun Yet?

you think heaven has a party when someone turns from sin to God? How do you feel about the statement "Christians are no fun?" Explain. How can knowing God give a reason to celebrate? What are ways people celebrate that God wouldn't approve of?

CLOSING

Have kids form a huddle and put their hands in the center.

Say: *Real fun is following God. If any of you want to know more about how to follow God, I'd love to talk to you about it after this meeting.*

Lead the group in a short prayer, thanking God for giving us a reason to celebrate. On "Amen," have kids shout in unison, "Real fun is following God!" Dismiss with a group hug.

Color Me Equal

■ **Theme:** Racism and prejudice
■ **Scripture:** Galatians 3:26-28
■ **Overview:** Kids will experience different treatment based on colors they wear.
■ **Preparation:** You'll need enough cookies for everyone and a Bible.

EXPERIENCE

Show kids the cookies and say: *You're such a great group, I brought you a surprise—cookies. Now let's eat up!*

Begin passing out cookies to group members. Each time you come to someone wearing green (or another color of your choice), refuse to give him or her a cookie and say: *Oh, you're wearing green. I hate green.*

Each time you come to someone wearing pink (or another color of your choice), give him or her two cookies and say: *All right! You're wearing pink. I love pink.*

After you've distributed the cookies, ask: *How did you feel as I passed out the cookies? Explain. How did you respond to my prejudiced attitude? How was the way I treated you like the way people treat each other in real life? How do you respond to prejudiced attitudes in real life?*

RESPONSE

Give cookies to kids who didn't get them earlier. Then have a volunteer read Galatians 3:26-28 aloud. Ask: *How was my attitude during cookie distribution different from the attitude of this passage? Based on this passage, how do you think God wants us to treat each other? If someone were to study our youth group, what would they say about our views toward racism and prejudice? Explain. How can we help each other exhibit the attitude of Galatians 3:26-28?*

CLOSING

Ask kids to commit to looking up information about a

Color Me Equal

different race or culture this week. Suggest they check their school or public libraries for reference materials. Tell kids you'll give them an opportunity to share what they learn at your next meeting.

Form a circle for closing prayer. Have kids fill in the blank with a positive quality about the person on their right as they say the following sentence prayer: "Thanks, Lord, for (student's name) unique quality of _____ ." Kids might fill in the blank with words like "helpfulness," "an encouraging attitude," or "accepting others."

Feeding the World— Next Door

■ **Theme:** Global compassion
■ **Scripture:** Matthew 25:31-46
■ **Overview:** Kids will experience what it's like to have a shortage of food.
■ **Preparation:** Prepare enough cooked rice, bread, and water for four average servings. You'll also need paper plates, plastic utensils, and Bibles.

EXPERIENCE

Divide the four servings of food among the entire group. Casually eat and enjoy the meal with the kids. Afterward, have kids form a circle and take turns sharing how they liked the meal. Explain that many families in the world must survive for days—and sometimes weeks—on this amount of food.

Ask: *How would you feel if this were all you had to eat today? for the week? What would you do if this were all your best friend's family had to eat?*

RESPONSE

Read Matthew 25:31-46 aloud and with expression. Then have kids form trios to discuss these questions. Have trio members take turns reporting their answers to the group.

Ask: *How does this parable make you feel about the hungry and poor of our world? Explain. Which characters do you relate to most in the parable? Why? What do you think is a Christian's responsibility toward global problems? What keeps us from fulfilling those responsibilities?*

CLOSING

Have trios brainstorm specific ways they can be like the sheep in the parable in the following areas: 1) in their church, 2) in their community, 3) in their nation, and 4) in the world.

Feeding the World— Next Door

For example, kids might deliver food to elderly shut-ins from the church, volunteer at community organizations that help the needy, participate in workcamps or service projects across the United States, or sponsor a child in a foreign country.

Have trios share their ideas with the group. Then gather kids together and kneel in the center of the room. As you pass a plastic spoon from person to person, have kids take turns saying sentence prayers for people in need all over the world.

Draw!

■ **Theme:** Discipling others
■ **Scripture:** 1 Thessalonians 5:11; Hebrews 3:13; 10:24-25
■ **Overview:** Group members will work together to draw a picture and compare that to helping each other grow closer to God.
■ **Preparation:** You'll need paper, pencils, chalk, a chalkboard, and Bibles.

EXPERIENCE

Form pairs and distribute paper and pencils to each group.

Say: *In your pairs, choose one person to be the artist and one person to describe the drawing.*

Have all the artists turn so their backs are to the chalkboard, then draw a bus on the board. Inform artists they must keep their backs to the board for the entire activity.

Say: *Describers, your job is to tell your partner how to draw what's on the board without telling him or her what it is, naming any elements of the drawing, or moving from the neck down. That means you can tell your partner where to place the pencil on the paper, and whether to draw lines or circles and the like, but no more. You have three minutes. Go.*

RESPONSE

After three minutes, have kids compare their drawings to the drawing on the board. Then have kids discuss the following questions in their pairs.

Ask: *What were you thinking about during this activity? How was this activity like the way we describe Jesus to others? What was easy or difficult in this activity? What's easy or hard about helping others strengthen their relationships with God?*

Gather the group together and have three volunteers read 1 Thessalonians 5:11; Hebrews 3:12-13; and Hebrews 10:24-25. Then ask: *Why do you think Jesus wants us to encourage each other to follow him? How does it make you feel when you communicate a good "picture" of Jesus to a friend? What are*

Draw!

specific ways we can follow the instructions of these verses this week?

CLOSING

Make sure everyone has a sheet of paper and a pencil. Have kids draw a new copy of your picture on the board and re-write Hebrews 10:24 in their own words at the top of their papers. Encourage kids to take their drawings and Scripture paraphrases home as a reminder to help others grow closer to God.

Inner Tube Dates

■ **Theme:** Dating
■ **Scripture:** 2 Corinthians 6:14-15
■ **Overview:** Students will examine how the differences in priorities Christians and non-Christians have can affect a dating relationship.
■ **Preparation:** Gather two old bicycle inner tubes (use one as a backup in case the other breaks) and two cones or markers for a race. You'll also need Bibles.

EXPERIENCE

Form two teams and have teams line up 15 feet from each other on one side of the room. Place a cone (or marker) about 25 feet from the front of each team line. Have the first players in each line pair up and stand inside the inner tube at an equal distance from both cones.

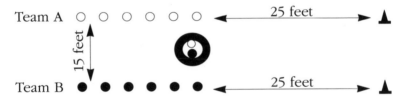

Team A ○ ○ ○ ○ ○ ○ ←————— 25 feet —————▶ ▲

Team B ● ● ● ● ● ● ←————— 25 feet —————▶ ▲

Say: *The object of this relay is to pull the opposing team member away from his or her team's cone and toward your team's cone. We'll take turns pairing up until every team member has had a chance to play. The team that reaches its cone the most times will be declared the winner. If one team member falls out of the tube, the opposing team will automatically win that round.*

Caution kids not to be too rough during the race. If a team member falls down but stays in the tube, pause the race until that person is standing again. After everyone has raced, declare a winner. Then have kids pair up with someone from the opposing team to discuss these questions.

Ask: *What feelings did you have during this race? How were the differences in goals like the differences in priorities that*

Inner Tube Dates

Christians and non-Christians have? How can those differences affect a dating relationship between a Christian and non-Christian?

RESPONSE

Have pairs read 2 Corinthians 6:14-15 and continue discussing these questions. Ask: *How does this Scripture apply to a dating relationship? What conflicting goals might Christians and non-Christians have? How could someone get "pulled off course" by not following the advice of 2 Corinthians 6:14-15 in a dating relationship?*

CLOSING

Form a circle and place the inner tube on the floor in the center. Have pairs take turns standing in the inner tube while the rest of the class prays the following prayer in unison for them: "Lord, we're thankful (students' names) have a lot to offer in a dating relationship. Help them choose wisely who they date. Amen."

One-Minute Teachers

■ **Theme:** Teachers
■ **Scripture:** Proverbs 8
■ **Overview:** Group members will commit to seek wisdom.
■ **Preparation:** You'll need Bibles, paper, pencils, newsprint, and a marker.

EXPERIENCE

Form two groups and say: *Today, instead of being students, you're going to become teachers. In your groups, read Proverbs 8 and come up with a one-minute lesson on wisdom to teach someone from the other group. Group 1, make your lesson fit the title "The Importance of Wisdom." Group 2, make your lesson fit the title "How to Get Wisdom." Ready? Go.*

Distribute paper and pencils to everyone and give groups four minutes to prepare their lessons. Then have kids choose a partner from the opposing group to form pairs. Give kids two minutes to "teach" their lessons to their partners.

RESPONSE

Have pairs join together to form groups of no more than four. Tell groups to assign one person to record their ideas, another to act as a representative who reports answers, a third to act as a reader, and a fourth to be an encourager who urges everyone to participate in the discussion.

Have groups discuss the following questions. Write them on newsprint so groups can refer back to them during discussions. Ask: *How did it feel to teach someone about wisdom? How was that like the way your teachers might feel? Who, besides teachers at school, are your teachers in life? How can teachers help you gain wisdom for living? How do you know when to believe what your teachers tell you?*

After a few minutes, have the representatives take turns telling how their groups responded.

One-Minute Teachers

CLOSING

Have kids think of the most influential teacher in their lives, such as a teacher at school or church, or a parent. Then, in their groups, have kids pray for those teachers.

Card Capers

■ **Theme:** Competition
■ **Scripture:** Proverbs 11:24-25
■ **Overview:** Group members will compare the results of competition and cooperation.
■ **Preparation:** You'll need 3×5 cards and Bibles.

EXPERIENCE

Form teams of no more than three and give each team 15 3×5 cards.

Say: *Let's see who can make the biggest card building in three minutes. As you're building, you can't touch anyone else's cards, but you can send one team member out to try to knock down other teams' buildings by blowing or shaking it. Go.*

Watch group members as they work. See how they react when their work is threatened. After three minutes have everyone display their buildings for the group. Then ask: *How did you feel during this activity? How was the way we competed to build card buildings like the way we compete in life?*

RESPONSE

Have teams read Proverbs 11:24-25. Say: *The instructions were "Let's see who can make the biggest card building." You didn't have to compete in this activity if you didn't want to.* Ask: *Did any of your teams work together to make a building? Why or why not? What would be the advantages of teams cooperating to build one big building instead of competing to build several smaller ones? How would that have reflected the attitude of Proverbs 11:24-25? What are the advantages of cooperating with others in real life? How can we put Proverbs 11:24-25 in practice this week?*

CLOSING

Have kids combine their cards and work together to build a new, larger, card building. Reward kids' efforts with a snack.

He Ain't Heavy

■ **Theme:** Friends
■ **Scripture:** Ecclesiastes 4:9-12; Proverbs 19:6
■ **Overview:** Group members will help each other reach a goal.
■ **Preparation:** You'll need enough candy for everyone to have a piece and Bibles.

EXPERIENCE

Have kids choose a partner for this activity and have pairs stand against one wall of the room.

Say: *Each of you has a broken right leg—you can't use it at all. In your pairs, work together to cross the room and touch the opposite wall. You can hop, crawl, or do whatever, as long as you don't use your right leg. Let's see if all pairs can make it across in two minutes or less. Ready? Go.*

Time kids as they cross the room. After two minutes, encourage kids to applaud themselves for their efforts.

RESPONSE

Have pairs read Ecclesiastes 4:9-12 and discuss these questions. After each question, have kids take turns reporting their answers to the group. Ask: *What feelings did you have during this activity? In what ways did your partner help you get across the room? How was Ecclesiastes 4:9-12 demonstrated in this activity? How was this activity like the way friends help each other in real life? What does it take to be a good friend like the ones described in Ecclesiastes 4:9-12? How can Jesus be your best friend in life?*

CLOSING

Have a person read Proverbs 19:6 aloud. Say: *The best gifts to give a friend aren't money or possessions. They're things like a listening ear, laughter, encouragement, or other positive qualities.*

Distribute candy to everyone. Have kids give their candy

He Ain't Heavy

to another person in the room, completing this sentence as they do: "One gift you have to offer new friends is _____ ." Tell kids to fill in the blank with a positive trait about the person receiving the candy, such as kindness, fun-loving attitude, or loyalty.

Common Denominators

- **Theme:** Other denominations
- **Scripture:** 1 Corinthians 1:10-13
- **Overview:** Students will examine differences and similarities between their church and other denominations.
- **Preparation:** You'll need a statement of faith from your church and a Bible.

EXPERIENCE

Say: *I'm going to call out various qualities; you'll have 10 seconds to find every other person who shares this quality with you.*

Read items from the following list and have students clump together with others who share that characteristic. Pause after each statement.

Say:

Find everyone whose favorite pizza topping is the same as yours.

Find everyone who is wearing the same color clothes as you are.

Find everyone who is wearing shoes like yours.

Find everyone who has the same favorite subject as yours.

Find everyone who believes your favorite music group is the best in the world.

Gather everyone back together. Have kids stand as you ask the following questions. Give kids a few seconds to think after each question. Tell group members you'd like to hear lots of interesting responses. When one person shares an answer, anyone who thought of the same answer and has nothing more to add can sit down. When everyone is seated, ask the next question and repeat the process.

Ask: *What did you like or dislike about this activity? Explain. How was this activity like the way people of similar faiths group together into denominations? How would you define a denomination? What denominations are represented*

Common Denominators

by churches in our city?

RESPONSE

Read several items from a your church's doctrinal statement. See if students can identify items where your church differs with other denominations. For example, your church may offer infant baptism while another doesn't.

Read 1 Corinthians 1:10-13 aloud. Ask: *How do you feel when other Christians don't share the same beliefs as you? Why do you think many Christians don't agree on faith issues? Is it ever OK for Christians to disagree about certain beliefs? Explain. What can you do this week to help Christians overcome denominational differences and follow the advice of Paul in 1 Corinthians 1:10-13?*

CLOSING

As a symbol of Christian unity, join hands and sing "We Are His Hands" or "I Love You With the Love of the Lord" to close. (Both songs are available in *The Group Songbook,* published by Group.)

World's Greatest Whiner

■ **Theme:** Complaining
■ **Scripture:** Philippians 2:14
■ **Overview:** Teenagers will compete for the honor of being named World's Greatest Whiner, then discuss alternatives to whining and complaining.
■ **Preparation:** You'll need an uncooked hot dog, a paper napkin, a flashlight, and a Bible.

EXPERIENCE

Form trios and have kids brainstorm things that cause them to whine or complain. Have each trio choose a representative whiner to report their group's complaints. Encourage the representative whiners to really ham up their reports by using their best whiny voices and actions. Pass the "whine-o-weenie microphone" (a hot dog wrapped in a napkin) from whiner to whiner to signify which group should report.

Invite kids to rate whiners by applauding after each report. Select a volunteer to serve as a "whine-o-meter." Have that volunteer place an elbow on an open palm and raise his or her forearm to indicate the strength of the applause for each whiner. Designate the top applause-getter as the World's Greatest Whiner and award him or her the whine-o-weenie microphone as a prize.

Then have kids discuss these questions in their trios: *What did you think of our whiners during this activity? How do you react to someone who's whining in real life? What do people hope to accomplish by whining? Does it work? Why or why not? Do you ever get annoyed at yourself for whining? Explain.*

RESPONSE

Bring everyone together and read Philippians 2:14-15 aloud.

Ask: *What changes would a candidate for World's Greatest*

World's Greatest Whiner

Whiner have to make to follow the instructions of this passage? Is it ever OK to whine? Explain. How can being a Christian help you overcome a desire to whine and complain? What alternative actions could you take when you're tempted to whine?

CLOSING

Turn off the lights and form a tight circle. Hold the flashlight under your chin and say, "I'm gonna shine, not whine." Hold the flashlight under the chin of the person on your left and have everyone in the group say, "(Name of person) is gonna shine, not whine." Continue in this manner, affirming everyone in the circle.

The Big Smear

■ **Theme:** Reputation
■ **Scripture:** Proverbs 22:1,4
■ **Overview:** Group members will compare a reputation to looking at a mirror covered with peanut butter.
■ **Preparation:** You'll need peanut butter, paper towels, glass cleaner, and a Bible. Arrange to have kids meet in an area with a large mirror, such as a restroom.

EXPERIENCE

Gather everyone in front of a large mirror. Pass around a jar of peanut butter and invite kids to smear peanut butter on the mirror. After everyone has participated in the big smear, ask: *How clearly can you see yourselves in this mirror? How is the way this peanut butter affects your reflection like the way a reputation affects how others see you? What kind of reputation do you want? How does that match with what God wants for you? What can you do to acquire a Godlike reputation?*

Allow a few moments for kids to wash their hands. Then distribute paper towels and glass cleaner and have kids work together to clean the mirror. As they clean, ask: *How could cleaning up this mirror affect our reputation as a group? How is cleaning this mirror like or unlike "cleaning up" a reputation?*

RESPONSE

Have kids sit in a circle on the floor. Pass around the peanut butter. Have kids each take a fingerful of peanut butter, then tell one thing that can ruin a person's reputation, such as gossip, lying, bragging, or hanging out with a wild crowd. Then go around the circle again. This time have kids eat their fingerful of peanut butter and tell one way to keep a good reputation or get rid of a bad one. Kids might say things like "Refuse to listen to gossip" or "Choose carefully who I hang out with."

The Big Smear

CLOSING

Read Proverbs 22:1,4 aloud. Ask: *Do you agree or disagree with these verses? Explain. Do these verses apply more to Christians than to other people? Why or why not?*

Close by giving everyone a paper towel to use as a reminder to keep their reputations clean.

Non-Trivial Pursuit

■ **Theme:** Listening
■ **Scripture:** James 1:19
■ **Overview:** Teenagers will listen carefully to questions in a pop quiz, then evaluate how carefully they listen in other situations.
■ **Preparation:** You'll need wrapped candies and Bibles.

EXPERIENCE

Say: *We're going to have a pop quiz on trivia. The first person to pop up and answer each question wins a piece of candy. If you pop up before I finish the question, you must finish the question correctly before giving the answer.*

Read the following questions slowly and deliberately so kids will attempt to jump early.

Ask:

When is Valentine's Day? (Feb. 14)

How many books are in the New Testament? (27)

Who was the first person to walk on the moon? (Neil Armstrong)

How many letters are there in the word "elephant"? (8)

What's the postal abbreviation for New Hampshire? (NH)

What's the name of the star ship in the original Star Trek TV series? (USS Enterprise)

What was President John Kennedy's middle name? (Fitzgerald)

RESPONSE

Ask: *On a scale of 1 to 10, with 10 being "all ears" and 1 being "deaf as a hammer," how carefully were you listening to me? What were the rewards of listening carefully to me? How was this like or unlike how carefully you listen to your parents? your teachers? your friends at school? What are the rewards of listening carefully? What are the consequences of not listening carefully? How do you feel when someone pays close attention to you when you're talking? How do you feel when someone you're talking to looks away or seems uninterested?*

Non-Trivial Pursuit

CLOSING

Say: *Form pairs and read James 1:19 together. Then take two minutes discuss with your partner why you agree or disagree with the statement "Listening is the simplest way to show love."*

Close with a minute of silent prayer. Tell kids to thank God for always listening and to ask God to help them be attentive, loving listeners.

You've Got It, but I Want It!

■ **Theme:** Jealousy
■ **Scripture:** James 4:1-7
■ **Overview:** Teenagers attempt to gain the most desirable prize in a game.
■ **Preparation:** On separate 3×5 cards write prize names such as a Corvette, graduating from college with straight A's, a mansion with an indoor pool, a tropical cruise every January for the rest of your life, an Olympic gold medal in the sport of your choice, a year's supply of Mountain Dew, an opportunity to guest star on your favorite TV program, being elected president of the United States, being drafted by your favorite NBA team, or winning the lottery. Make enough prize cards for every person to have one. You'll also need Bibles.

EXPERIENCE

Have kids sit in a circle. Lay the prize cards face down in front of you. Say: *We're going to play a game called Draw or Trade. First I'll take a prize card and read my prize aloud. Then we'll go around the circle to the right. When it's your turn, you may either take a prize that someone has already drawn, or draw one of the prize cards that's still face down. If you take someone else's card, that person gets to draw a new prize card. When we get around the circle, the game ends, and there won't be any more swapping.*

As you play, imagine you actually will receive the prize you end up with. Choose the prize you'd most enjoy winning in real life.

Draw a card and read the first prize aloud. Then ask the person on your right whether he or she wants to take your prize or draw a new prize card. Continue until everyone has a card.

You've Got It, but I Want It!

RESPONSE

As you ask the following questions, give kids a few seconds to think after each question, and tell them you'd like to hear lots of interesting responses. Have kids hold their cards on their foreheads to signal when they're ready to share an answer. After one person shares an answer, anyone who thought of the same answer and has nothing more to add should lower his or her card. When all cards are lowered, ask the next question and repeat the process.

Ask: *How do you feel about the prize you ended up with? How did you feel when someone took away a prize you wanted to keep? How is that like the way you feel when someone gets something you want in real life?*

Read James 4:1-7 aloud. Ask: *How was our game a negative example of this Scripture? Is it easy or hard for you to live out the last part of this passage? Explain. How do feelings of jealousy affect a relationship? How do they affect you? How can we help each other live out the positive qualities described in this passage?*

CLOSING

Have kids form pairs. Say: *Tell your partner one way you struggle with jealousy, then discuss how to overcome those feelings.* Allow two or three minutes for sharing. Then encourage kids to swap prize cards and keep them as a reminder not to be jealous but to rejoice with those who rejoice.

Generation Gap

~~~~~~

■ **Theme:** Grandparents
■ **Scripture:** Proverbs 16:31
■ **Overview:** Kids will "age" a volunteer, then discuss how to relate to older people.
■ **Preparation:** Gather a sheer ladies' scarf, a 2-foot length of twine, and a 20-pound sack of potatoes. You'll also need a Bible.

EXPERIENCE

Recruit a volunteer to become a grandparent. Have other students "age" the volunteer by tying the sheer scarf around his or her eyes, tying the twine loosely around his or her ankles, and balancing the 20-pound sack of potatoes on the volunteer's bent back.

Have everyone (including the aged person) walk briskly around the room. When you reach the starting point, reverse directions and do another lap of the room. Next, have everyone take off their shoes and put them back on. Finally, pass a Bible around the group and ask each person to read, in order, one word of Proverbs 16:31 (repeat the verse as necessary).

RESPONSE

Sit in a circle to discuss the following questions. Have kids take turns sharing their responses with the group. Ask: *How did it feel to watch our volunteer struggle to do the same things the rest of us were doing with ease? How are the disabilities we created for our volunteer like what happens to people as they grow old? How does Proverbs 16:31 imply older people should be treated? How does our culture treat older people? How do you feel about the way we treat older people in our church and in our families?*

CLOSING

Read Proverbs 16:31 again. Say: *The Bible teaches us that older people deserve our respect. Pair up and tell your partner*

Generation Gap

the name of an older person you have contact with and what you will do this week to show that person acceptance and respect.

10-Minute
Devotions on
Faith Issues

We're Not in Kansas Anymore

▰▰▰▰▰▰▰▰▰▰▰▰▰▰▰▰▰▰▰▰▰▰▰▰▰▰

- **Theme:** The kingdom of God
- **Scripture:** Colossians 1:11-14; Revelation 21:1-6
- **Overview:** Teenagers will examine what it means to be a citizen of the kingdom of God.
- **Preparation:** Photocopy and cut out enough passports from the "Passports" handout (p. 68) for every student to have one. You'll also need snacks for everyone, pencils, and Bibles.

EXPERIENCE

Give each person one of the four passports from the "Passports" handout (p. 68) and tell kids not to let anyone else see their passports. Be sure to distribute roughly the same number of each passport. If you have six or fewer in your group, use only two of the passports.

Say: *You're now a citizen of the country listed on your passport. When I turn out the lights, we'll see how long it takes for everyone to link arms with their fellow citizens. While the lights are out, you can't tell what country you're from or show anyone your passport. The only way others will know which country you're from is by the way you act. Refer to your passport for hints on how citizens from your country act. When all citizens are linked up, we'll have a snack as a reward.*

Turn off the lights and have kids link up by country. After all countries are linked up, turn on the lights and award snacks to everyone. Then have kids join with citizens of other countries to form groups of no more than four. Have groups discuss the following questions, one at a time, and take turns reporting their answers to the large group.

Ask: *What would it be like to actually be a citizen of the country on your passport? How did your actions reveal your country of origin for this activity? What do actions reveal about people in real life? What would your actions have been during this activity if the kingdom of God had been listed as your country of citizenship?*

We're Not in Kansas Anymore

RESPONSE

Have groups read Colossians 1:11-14 and discuss these questions. Ask: *How do the rewards of being a citizen of the kingdom of God compare to the rewards of our activity? How can we become citizens of the kingdom of God? How can we reflect in our actions that we're citizens of the kingdom of God this week? What's hard about living as a citizen of the kingdom of God? How can we help each other overcome these obstacles this week?*

CLOSING

Gather everyone in a circle and distribute pencils. Read Revelation 21:1-6 aloud. Then have kids each draw a picture on their passports that reflects their feelings about God's future reward for citizens of his kingdom. For example, kids might draw a smiley face to represent happiness, or a bird soaring through the air to represent freedom. (Tell kids it's OK to use stick figures in their drawings.)

Then have kids write this sentence on their passports and fill in the blank with their own thoughts: "Because I'm a citizen of heaven, this week I'll _____ ." Kids might write, "I'll tell others about heaven," "I'll thank God for my future," or "I'll try to be more like God." Have kids take their passports home as reminders of their heavenly citizenship.

Passports

Passport holder's country of origin:
The Federation of Chocolate Lovers

Citizens' favorite phrase:
"Say, is that chocolate?"

Citizens' favorite activity:
Eating

Passport holder's country of origin:
The United District of Athletes

Citizens' favorite phrase:
"Play ball!"

Citizens' favorite activity:
Doing jumping jacks

Passport holder's country of origin:
The Kingdom of Melodia

Citizens' favorite phrase:
"I feel a song coming on!"

Citizens' favorite activity:
Singing "Happy Birthday"

Passport holder's country of origin:
The Nursery Nation

Citizens' favorite phrase:
"I want my mommy!"

Citizens' favorite activity:
Crying

Highway to Hell

- **Theme:** Hell
- **Scripture:** Luke 16:19-31; 2 Peter 3:9
- **Overview:** Teenagers will examine the parable of the rich man and Lazarus for warnings about hell.
- **Preparation:** You'll need newsprint, markers, cellophane tape, snacks, and Bibles.

EXPERIENCE

In pairs, have kids read Luke 16:19-31. Tell one student in each pair to read the passage, and the other to summarize what's read.

Then give each pair a sheet of newsprint and markers. Say: *Let's imagine we have access to the "road of life" the rich man in this parable traveled. In your pairs, create a warning sign on the road of life that would've helped this man change his eternal fate. For example, your sign might say: "Warning! Serve God, Not Money!" You've got three minutes. Go.*

After everyone is finished, have kids tape their signs all over the room. Then have kids form a single-file line behind you. Tell kids to pretend to drive a sports car as you lead them on a "road trip" around the room to read the signs. Stop at each sign and have its creators explain why their message would be important for the rich man to hear.

Halfway through the road trip, pause and shout: *Duck!* Drop to the floor and cover your head. Give a snack to anyone who heeded your warning and joined you on the floor. Then finish the road trip.

RESPONSE

After reading all the signs, lead the group to the center of the room. Have kids stand as you ask the following questions one at a time. Tell the group you'd like to hear lots of interesting responses. After each question, when one person shares an answer, anyone who thought of the same answer and has nothing more to add may sit down. When all kids are seated, ask the next question and repeat the process.

Highway to Hell

Ask: *When have you felt like the rich man in this parable? When have you felt like Lazarus? What were your thoughts when I warned everyone to duck? What are your thoughts about hell? How would you have responded if you'd been the rich man and read our warning signs? What warnings about hell do people today need to hear? How does your response when I shouted "duck!" compare to how people today respond to warnings about hell?*

Have group members answer the next questions silently instead of aloud: *What warnings about hell do you need to hear? What will you do in response to those warnings?*

CLOSING

Read aloud 2 Peter 3:9. Say: *God doesn't want us to end up like the rich man in this parable. After our prayer, I'd be glad to talk to any of you who want to know how to avoid the rich man's fate.*

Close with a prayer of thanks to Jesus for providing the way to escape hell. Then make yourself available to share with kids individually how to receive God's gift of eternal life.

Changing Values

■ **Theme:** Values
■ **Scripture:** Matthew 16: 24-26; John 3:16
■ **Overview:** Teenagers will examine the hidden value of water and compare it to a relationship with Jesus.
■ **Preparation:** You'll need a bottle of water; a $20 bill; two tickets to a popular event such as a basketball game, concert, or movie; and cups. You'll also need Bibles.

EXPERIENCE

Show everyone the water, the money, and the tickets. Say: *Rank these items according to their value to you. Rank the most valuable as #1 and the least valuable as #3. Go.*

Send everyone who ranked the water first to the north side of the room, everyone who ranked the money first to the east side, and everyone who ranked the tickets first to the south side. Then have volunteers from each group tell what makes their item valuable enough to be ranked first.

Then say: *I forgot to tell you one little thing. You're going on a weeklong trip to the desert, and the only thing you can take with you is your top-ranked item. That means anyone who chose the water will survive and the rest of you won't.*

Ask: *Now how do you feel about your rankings? Why does something as simple as water become so valuable when survival is at stake? How is a relationship with Jesus like water?*

RESPONSE

Form groups of no more than three and have the person wearing the most blue in each trio read Matthew 16:24-26. Ask: *How is gaining the world but losing your soul like having lots of money in the middle of a desert? What does this passage suggest is most valuable in life? How does your life reflect the things you value most? What changes are needed to make your relationship with Jesus the most valuable part of your life?*

Changing Values

CLOSING

Read John 3:16 aloud and say: *This verse makes it clear what God values most: us! Let's drink a toast to God to say thanks.*

Pour everyone a cup of water. Then have kids raise their cups as you say: *To God, whose love makes us valuable forever!*

Turn Up the Heat

- ■ **Theme:** Worship
- ■ **Scripture:** Ezekiel 36:25-27; John 4:23-24
- ■ **Overview:** Group members will explore how God can use worship to soften their hearts.
- ■ **Preparation:** You'll need ice cubes for everyone, paper cups, paper towels, a small prize (such as a discount coupon for the next youth event), and Bibles.

EXPERIENCE

Form a circle and give everyone a paper cup and an ice cube. Say: *When I say "go," work as quickly as you can to melt your ice cube and fill your cup with water. You may use only your hands to melt your ice cube. Go.*

Award the prize to the first person to completely melt his or her ice cube. Then give kids paper towels to dry off with, and ask: *What thoughts went through your mind during this contest? How were the ice cubes in our activity like cold, or hardened, hearts? How does the warmth of our hands on an ice cube compare to the warmth of God's Spirit on a cold, hardened heart?*

RESPONSE

Form pairs and have kids read Ezekiel 36:25-27 and John 4:23-24. In their pairs, have kids discuss these questions one at a time and take turns sharing their responses with the group. Ask: *How does worshiping God allow God's Spirit to warm our hearts? What happens when we allow God's Spirit to melt our hearts through worship? In what ways can people worship God in spirit and truth? How can worshiping God in spirit and truth "fill the cups" of our lives? How can we encourage one another to worship God this week?*

CLOSING

Close by singing worship songs such as "A Perfect Heart" and "Change My Heart, Oh God." Both songs are available in *The Group Songbook.*

Wet Head?

■ **Theme:** Peace
■ **Scripture:** John 14:27; Philippians 4:6-7; Colossians 3:15
■ **Overview:** Group members will discuss how to experience God's peace in pressure situations.
■ **Preparation:** You'll need an outdoor area or an indoor area that may get wet. You'll also need water balloons, a plastic garbage bag for everyone, paper towels, and Bibles.

EXPERIENCE

Form pairs and give each pair one water balloon and two plastic garbage bags. Have kids tear holes for their heads and arms in the bags and wear the bags as coverings over their clothes.

In an outdoor area (or an indoor area that may get wet) have partners stand 10 feet apart and toss their balloons back and forth to each other. After each successful toss, have partners take one large step backward and repeat the process. If a toss is unsuccessful, have kids stay where they were when their balloons broke until everyone is finished. See which pair can toss its balloon the farthest without allowing it to break.

Afterward, pass out paper towels for kids to dry off with, and have pairs join together to form groups of no more than four. Direct kids to number off within their groups from one to four, and say: *Discuss the next question in your groups. Then I'll call out a number from one to four. The person in your group whose number I call out will be responsible for sharing your group's answer. Repeat the process for each question.*

Ask: *How did you feel during this activity? Explain. When do you feel like that in real life? How do you respond to pressure situations in real life?*

RESPONSE

Have each person in each foursome read one of the following scriptures aloud: John 14:27; Philippians 4:6; Philippians 4:7; and Colossians 3:15. Ask: *How can these verses*

Wet Head?

encourage us when pressure situations make us feel like popped water balloons? How can God's peace help us respond to stressful circumstances? How does God give us peace? How can we seek God's peace in our lives?

CLOSING

Form a circle and hand one person a water balloon. Have kids take turns holding the balloon and completing this sentence: "One thing I've learned today that can keep my life from getting 'soaked' this week is _____ ." Kids might say things such as "God's peace is available to me," or "God's peace can help me face stressful circumstances."

Paper Wad Persecution

- **Theme:** Persecution
- **Scripture:** Matthew 5:10-12
- **Overview:** Kids will experience persecution and discuss how to face opposition to their faith.
- **Preparation:** You'll need one roll of masking tape for every five group members, old newspapers, newsprint, a marker, and Bibles.

EXPERIENCE

Form groups of no more than five and distribute masking tape and newspaper to the groups. Have each group choose one volunteer to be wrapped in masking tape, sticky side out. Then have the rest of the group wrap the volunteer. (Tell kids not to wrap tape on their volunteers' heads.) Next, have group members form a circle around their volunteers and gently toss wads of newspaper at their volunteers' taped torsos. The paper wads will stick to the tape, covering the volunteer in newspaper.

RESPONSE

After a few minutes, have groups sit in circles and discuss these questions. Write the questions on newsprint so kids can refer to them during their discussions. Ask: *How did it feel to be the volunteer in this activity? How did it feel to attack the volunteer with paper wads? How was this activity like or unlike the way Christians are sometimes attacked for their beliefs?*

Have the person in each group who lives the farthest from the church read Matthew 5:10-12 aloud. Then ask: *How do you feel when others attack you or your friends because of your Christian faith? In what ways do people attack the Christian faith? How do you respond to those attacks? How do you think Jesus would respond in those same situations? How can we help each other stand firm in the face of opposition to our faith this week?*

Paper Wad Persecution

CLOSING

Have group members help their volunteers remove the tape and paper wads. Say: *Matthew 5:12 says we can rejoice when we face opposition to our faith, so let's do that right now.*

Have kids tear up their paper wads to make confetti. Then, on the count of three, have everyone throw the confetti in the air and shout, "Yea, God!"

Prayer: Today's Teenagers' Version

■ **Theme:** Prayer
■ **Scripture:** Matthew 6:9-13 (Lord's Prayer)
■ **Overview:** Group members will practice personalizing their prayers using Matthew 6:9-13 as a guide.
■ **Preparation:** You'll need paper, pencils, and Bibles.

EXPERIENCE

Form groups of no more than four and distribute paper and pencils to each group member. Say: *You've been chosen to translate the Bible into "Today's Teenagers' Version." Your first assignment for the TTV Bible is Matthew 6:9-13. In your groups, read this passage about prayer and "translate" it into words any teenager would understand and find meaningful. Be creative and work as a team, but make sure you each have a copy of your translated prayer. You have five minutes. Go.*

After five minutes, have kids number off within their groups from one to four. Form four new groups by sending all ones, twos, threes, and fours to different areas of the room. Have kids take turns praying their previous groups' translations aloud.

RESPONSE

Gather everyone together and have kids sit down as you ask the following questions. Tell group members you'd like to hear lots of interesting responses. When one person shares an answer, have anyone who thought of the same answer and has nothing more to add fold his or her hands (like children do when they pray). When all hands are folded, ask the next question and repeat the process.

Ask: *How did you feel as you heard and prayed personalized versions of the Lord's Prayer? How is that like or unlike the way you feel when you pray in real life? What can you learn from your TTV translation of Matthew 6:9-13 to help you in your daily prayer life? Why do you think God values prayer?*

Prayer: Today's Teenagers' Version

CLOSING

Use Matthew 6:9-13 as a guide for a closing prayer. As you say the Lord's Prayer line by line, pause and have kids respond by praying the corresponding line of their groups' "Today's Teenagers' Version" of the passage.

For example, you might read, "Our Father in Heaven," and some group members might respond, "Dear Dad, you're so much bigger than us ..." For this prayer, let kids know it's all right if their responsive words aren't exactly the same.

Munchie Mania

■ **Theme:** Poverty
■ **Scripture:** Proverbs 21:13; 22:16
■ **Overview:** Teenagers will experience what it feels like to never have quite enough.
■ **Preparation:** You'll need 10 different unbreakable items (such as a trash can, several different-colored Frisbees, a basketball, a football, a baseball, and a pillow), a bag of small candy bars, a whistle, newsprint, marker, and Bibles.

EXPERIENCE

Say: *Let's play a game.*

Form two to four teams of equal size. Line up the teams on opposite walls of the room. Place the 10 unbreakable items in the center of the room. Assign one item a value of 3,000 points, three items a value of 1,000 points each, and six items a value of 500 points each.

Show the teams the bag of candy bars. Advise kids that the object of this game is to gain enough points to "buy" the bag of candy bars for their teams. They'll gain points in each round of the game, and the first team to get 20,000 points will win the candy bars.

Explain that for each round of the game, you'll call out one characteristic, such as "people with blue socks" or "everyone wearing red," and then blow a whistle. At the sound of the whistle, those who possess that characteristic will try to grab as many of the items as possible from the center of the room and take them back to their team's wall. Add up the point values for the items collected by each team.

Say: *There's one catch: inflation. Every two rounds the cost of the candy bars will go up, so the sooner you buy them, the better. Ready? Let's play!*

Play several rounds, raising the cost of the candy bars 8,000 points every two rounds. See if any team is able to get enough points to buy the candy bars. Watch for reactions of the team members each time you raise the price.

After the game ask: *What did you think of this game? Explain. How might this game be like the way a needy person*

Munchie Mania

faces life? How did you feel each time the price of the candy bars went up? What would you do if your family suddenly found itself unable to buy food or pay for a place to live?

RESPONSE

Have kids form pairs and read Proverbs 21:13 and 22:16 to each other. Have pairs discuss these questions one at a time and take turns sharing responses with the whole group. Ask: *Judging from Proverbs 21:13 and 22:16, what's God's attitude toward people who are unable to have all their needs met? What's your attitude? Why do you think God allows poverty in the world? Why do you think God wants Christians to care for the needy?*

CLOSING

Write the following statistics on newsprint:

● More than one-third of the world's population (over two billion people) survives on a yearly income of only $200.

● In the United States alone, an estimated 1.2 million teenagers are homeless.

● More than 40 million people a year die of hunger and hunger-related diseases.

Ask kids to reflect silently on these statistics. Then have partners pray for each other to be a part of God's solution to poverty in the world.

Pizza Power

■ **Theme:** Disappointment
■ **Scripture:** Job 1; Psalm 33:20-22
■ **Overview:** Group members will experience
disappointment by having pizza served in a trash can.
■ **Preparation:** You'll need a trash can, pizza, self-stick
note pads, pencils, and Bibles. Make sure the inside of the
trash can is thoroughly clean and disinfected. If you're able,
use a new trash can for this experience. Smudge the outside
of the trash can with dirt or grease to make it appear dirty.

EXPERIENCE

Form a circle, show group members the pizza, and say: *I
decided we all deserved a little treat today, so I brought pizza
for everyone! Take a piece as I pass it around.*

Dump the pizza out of its box and into the trash can.
Then pass the can around and see if anyone takes a piece of
pizza. Afterward, explain that the trash can is actually clean and
disinfected inside, so it's safe to eat the pizza. Pass the pizza
around the circle again.

As kids enjoy the pizza, ask: *What feelings did you have
when I dumped the pizza in this trash can? Explain. How was
this experience like disappointing situations you face in real
life? How were your reactions to seeing the pizza dumped in the
trash can like or unlike the way you react to disappointment in
real life?*

RESPONSE

Form pairs and have kids read Job 1. Have one partner
read the passage, and the other summarize it. Tell partners to
switch roles every four verses.

Have pairs discuss the following questions one at a time.
After each question, have partners take turns reporting the
results of their discussions.

Ask: *What thoughts went through your mind as you read
the story of Job? How does your disappointment about the pizza
compare to Job's disappointments in this passage? What*

Pizza Power

disappointments does a normal high school student like you face? How would your reaction to disappointing circumstances compare to Job's? What can we learn from Job to help us deal with disappointment this week?

CLOSING

Distribute self-stick note pads and pencils to everyone. Have kids each write one disappointing situation they're facing on a self-stick note and paste it to their foreheads. Then read aloud Psalm 33:20-22 as an encouragement to the group. Next, have kids write Psalm 33:20 on a new self-stick note. Have kids paste their scriptures on their partners' heads and say to each other, "Our hope is in the Lord!"

Encourage group members to take their self-stick note scriptures home as reminders that hope is possible even in disappointing circumstances.

Candy, Anyone?

- **Theme:** The Bible
- **Scripture:** Psalm 119:97-105
- **Overview:** Group members will compare how they choose candy to how they approach reading the Bible.
- **Preparation:** Bring one or more boxes of assorted chocolates. You'll also need newsprint, a marker, and Bibles.

EXPERIENCE

Pass the assorted chocolates around the group. Challenge group members to pick one containing coconut. After everyone has a piece of candy, have them bite into their chocolates at the same time.

Award an extra piece of candy to those who chose a chocolate with coconut. Disqualify any who poked, broke, or otherwise adjusted the candy to see what was inside.

RESPONSE

As group members enjoy their candy, ask: *How did you decide which candy to choose? What would've happened if we'd never bitten into our candies? What were the results of biting into our candies? In what ways do people approach the Bible like we approached the chocolates in this activity? What happens to our faith when we "bite into" the Bible like we bit into the candies?*

CLOSING

Have group members call out positive words to describe their favorite candy as you write them on newsprint. Then form pairs and have kids read Psalm 119:97-105. Have pairs compare the words David uses to describe God's Word with the words they used to describe candy.

Say: *God's Word is better than any candy because it gives nourishment to our spiritual lives. Take your candy wrappers home as a reminder to "bite into" the sweet treasures found in the Bible.*

Welcome Back!

■ **Theme:** The return of Christ
■ **Scripture:** 1 Thessalonians 4:13-18
■ **Overview:** Group members will decorate the room for an important visitor and discuss the coming return of Jesus.
■ **Preparation:** Bring party decorations such as streamers, confetti, and balloons; and party snacks like mini-sandwiches, cookies, and punch. In addition, you might want to bring a cassette of upbeat Christian music and a cassette player. You'll also need a Bible.

EXPERIENCE

Give kids the party decorations and say: *We have a very special visitor coming today, so let's decorate the room to prepare for his coming.*

Turn on the music while kids decorate. If group members ask you who's coming, tell them it's a surprise and to keep decorating.

After the room is ready, form a circle and have kids take turns answering these questions: *What feelings do you have about having a special visitor here? What other preparations could we make to be ready for our visitor?*

RESPONSE

Say: *Well, I have good news and better news. The good news is that our visitor is already here among us. He lives in the hearts of Christians—he is Jesus. The better news is that one day soon he's coming physically to take his followers to heaven forever.*

Have someone wearing red shoes read 1 Thessalonians 4:13-18 aloud for the group. Then ask: *What feelings do you have about Jesus' return described in this passage? How can we "decorate" our lives in preparation for his coming? How can you know if you'll be going with Jesus to heaven when he returns? What can you do this week to help someone else "decorate" for Jesus' return?*

Welcome Back!

CLOSING

Bring out the party foods and say: *Since our visitor is here in spirit, let's go ahead and celebrate his coming physical return.*

Pass out the snacks and enjoy the celebration.

Confused?

■ **Theme:** Confusion
■ **Scripture:** Psalm 119:34, 99, 144, 169; James 1:5
■ **Overview:** Kids will discover God offers guidance for confusing situations.
■ **Preparation:** You'll need two chairs, one ball of any kind, and Bibles.

EXPERIENCE

Form two teams—team 1 and team 2. Have teams sit on opposite ends of the room with a "team chair" anywhere on each side.

Hold up a ball and say: *In this game, the goal is to get the ball away from the opposing team and onto your team's chair. I didn't have a chance to make up any rules, so I'm leaving that to you.*

Give each team two minutes to create five rules for the game, such as "Everyone must walk backward," or "You can carry the ball only between your knees." Have a representative from each team quickly explain his or her team's rules, telling kids to listen closely as this will be the only time the rules will be explained. Then toss the ball into the middle of the room and say: *We're playing with team 1's rules. Go!*

Every 30 seconds, change the rules by yelling: *Now we're using Team 2's rules!* or *Play by Team 1's rules now!*

After several minutes of play, end the game and ask which team won.

RESPONSE

Have kids choose a partner from the opposing team to discuss the following questions. Have pairs report their answers to the group after each question.

Ask: *What did you think of this game? Explain. How well were you able to remember all the rules? What was most confusing about the game? How was the confusion of this game like confusing situations in life? How do you respond in these situations? How do you respond when you feel confused about God?*

Confused?

Have pairs read Psalm 119:34, 99, 144, and 169. Ask: *Judging from these verses, how did the author of Psalm 119 respond to confusion in life? What can we learn from the author's response? How can God help you gain understanding? Why is understanding important?*

CLOSING

Read James 1:5 aloud. Say: *When life gets confusing like our game, we can turn to God for guidance and understanding.*

Close by having kids take turns completing this prayer: "Lord, please give me wisdom and understanding when I'm confused about _____ ." Kids might fill in the blank by saying things like, "my homework," "how to spend my time," or "my relationships with friends and family."

Do It!

■ **Theme:** Hypocrisy
■ **Scripture:** James 1:22-25
■ **Overview:** Group members will act out the opposite of their words and discuss the problem of hypocrisy.
■ **Preparation:** You'll need Bibles.

EXPERIENCE

Say: *We're going to play a game similar to Simon Says. Every time I read a command I want you to immediately repeat it out loud, but at the same time do the opposite of the command. For example, if I say, "Stand up," you should say, "Stand up" as you actually sit down. Anyone who does what they say, is out.*

Have kids stand. Read from the following list and have kids who do what they say sit down. The faster you read, the more difficult this game will become. Say:

Raise your right leg.
Turn in a circle counterclockwise.
Face the back of the room.
Stand up then sit down.
Scratch your left ear.
Walk slowly around the room.
Wave to the person on your right.
Shake your neighbor's left hand.
Open your eyes.
Recite the alphabet from A to Z.

RESPONSE

Afterward, congratulate any kids still standing, then ask: *What made this game confusing? How did it feel to say one thing then do another? What's your opinion of people who say one thing but do another in real life?*

Have kids form trios and read James 1:22-25 in their groups. Have trios discuss the following questions one at a time. Have a representative from each trio share his or her group's responses after discussing each question.

Ask: *Why do some people have trouble living out what they*

Do It!

say they believe? How can you tell what a person really believes? How is a person who forgets his or her reflection like someone whose actions don't reflect his or her words?

CLOSING

Say: *Let's practice making our words match our actions.*

Play the same game as before, but this time have kids do exactly what you say. Use the following list as your guide. Say:

Join with three others and have a group hug.

Find a partner and share one reason you're glad that person's part of our group.

Find a new partner and pray together, thanking God for your partner.

And Mercy for All

- **Theme:** Mercy
- **Scripture:** Romans 3:23-26; 6:23
- **Overview:** Group members will be treated with mercy and compare that experience to God's mercy.
- **Preparation:** You'll need small prizes such as candy bars, a bucket containing several water balloons, a pin, and Bibles.

EXPERIENCE

Say: *I'll give a prize to the first person who can quote Romans 6:23 without looking at a Bible. Everyone else will get doused with water balloons.*

Award a small prize to the first person to quote the verse. (It's OK if no one is able to.) Then hold up the water balloons and say: *Now, for those of you who didn't say the verse, it's time for your punishment.*

Wait for kids to respond. Then put the balloons down and say: *Nah. I care too much about you all to see you get soaking wet today. In fact, I think I'll give everyone a reward instead.*

Use the pin to pop the balloons in the bucket, then distribute the small prizes to everyone.

RESPONSE

Form two circles, one within the other. Have the inner circle face outward, and the outer circle face inward. Have kids pair up with the person in front of them, read Romans 3:23-26 and 6:23, and discuss this question: *How did it make you feel when you found out you were going to be pelted with water balloons? Explain.*

Have pairs share their answers with the group. Then tell kids on the inside circle to rotate one space to the right and form new pairs to discuss the next question. Repeat this process for each remaining question.

Ask: *How did you feel when you received a reward instead of punishment? How were my merciful actions in this activity like or unlike God's in real life? Why did Jesus have to die in our*

And Mercy for All

place? How does Jesus' merciful sacrifice affect your everyday life?

Have kids answer the next question silently. Ask: *Will God justly punish me for my wrong actions, or will I go free because of my faith in Jesus?*

CLOSING

Have kids stand and read Romans 6:23 aloud in unison. Then have kids take turns completing this sentence: "One word that describes my feelings about this verse is _____ ." Kids might say, "relieved," "grateful," or "unsure."

Close with a prayer of thanks for God's merciful gift to all who place their faith in Jesus. Afterward, make yourself available to answer questions group members might have about how to place their faith in Jesus.

10-Minute
Devotions for
Special Occasions

You Can't Get There From Here

■ **Theme:** New Year holiday
■ **Scripture:** 2 Corinthians 5:17
■ **Overview:** Group members will discover that where they end up depends a lot on where they start.
■ **Preparation:** Bring a banana, a six-pack of soft drinks, cups, five pennies, a dozen cookies, and a cup of dirt. You'll also need Bibles.

EXPERIENCE

Tell kids you're thinking of a number between one and five, and have them do the same.

Then say: *Add 12 to your number.* Pause. *Subtract three.* Pause. *Multiply by two.* Pause. *Add seven.* Pause. *Subtract five.* Pause. *Multiply by 10.* Pause. *Add 13.* Pause. *Subtract four.*

Have students form groups with others who ended up with the same answer.

Say: *Now, I have prizes for each group!*

Distribute one of the following items to each group: a banana, a six-pack of soft drinks and cups, five pennies, a dozen cookies, and a cup of dirt. Give the first item to the group that came up with the lowest number, the second item to the group that came up with the second lowest number, and so on. (If you have four groups, don't award the pennies. If you have three groups, don't award the pennies or the banana. If you have two groups, award only the cup of dirt and the soft drinks.)

RESPONSE

Have each group discuss the following questions and select a representative to share its answers with the large group. Ask the questions one at a time and have kids report answers after each question.

Ask: *How do you feel about the group you ended up in? Explain. What determined the group you ended up in? How do beginnings affect endings in real life?*

You Can't Get There From Here

Have everyone read 2 Corinthians 5:17 aloud in unison. Ask: *How can we use the start of a new year to allow God to give us a new beginning in life? How can allowing God to make us new at the beginning of the year affect where we end up at the end of the year? How can we make following God more than just a New Year's resolution that gets broken in a few weeks?*

CLOSING

Have students think of one goal they have for their spiritual lives in the coming year, such as reading the Bible regularly, serving in the church, or telling friends about Jesus. Then form pairs and have kids tell their partners their goals.

Say: *Let's start this year off right—with prayer. Take a minute to pray for your partner to be able to fulfill his or her goal over the course of this next year.*

At the Candy Factory

■ **Theme:** Valentine's Day
■ **Scripture:** 1 Corinthians 13:1-7
■ **Overview:** Group members will make new messages for a candy-heart factory and discuss 1 Corinthians 13:1-7.
■ **Preparation:** Bring pencils, enough heart-shaped papers for everyone in the group, and a bag of candy hearts. You'll also need Bibles.

EXPERIENCE

Form groups of no more than five and give each group five heart-shaped papers and pencils.

Say: *Your group has just taken a job at a candy-heart factory. Your first assignment is to create five new messages to be printed on candy hearts. Remember, space is limited, so your messages can't be more than three words each. You've got three minutes to come up with your ideas, or you'll be demoted to washing executives' cars. Ready? Go.*

After three minutes, flash the lights to regain group members' attention. Then give kids 30 seconds to tell their candy-heart messages to as many people as they can. Afterward, applaud the group for its creativity.

RESPONSE

Re-form the groups of no more than five. Have groups read 1 Corinthians 13:1-7 and discuss these questions one at a time. After discussions, have members of each group take turns reporting their answers to the large group. Each time a group reports an answer, toss its members a handful of candy hearts to share.

Ask: *How did you feel during this activity? Explain. How were your feelings during this activity like or unlike your feelings during the Valentine's season? How would Valentine's Day candy-heart messages be different if they reflected 1 Corinthians 13:1-7? If God were to send a candy-heart message to you for Valentine's Day, what would it be? How does that compare to the spoken and unspoken messages people hear*

At the Candy Factory

during the Valentine's season? How can we reflect God's messages of 1 Corinthians 13:1-7 to others during this Valentine's season?

CLOSING

To close, give each student three more candy hearts. Tell kids to give the hearts to three other people, either in the youth group, at home, or in the church. As they give away their hearts, tell them to say, "Thanks for the love you show me all year round."

Death of the Firstborn

■ **Theme:** Passover
■ **Scripture:** Revelation 5:9-10
■ **Overview:** Teenagers will simulate the death of the firstborn and examine how Jesus became their Passover lamb.
■ **Preparation:** You'll need Bibles.

EXPERIENCE

Form groups of no more than five and have each group form a circle. Tell kids you'll be talking about a serious topic and you'd like them to approach the devotion with a serious attitude.

Then say: *During the time when the Israelites were slaves in Egypt, God wanted to convince the Pharaoh of Egypt to free the Israelites. So, God declared that the firstborn son in each family would die as a result of Pharaoh's disobedience in not releasing the Israelites. Right now, find out who the oldest person in your group is.*

Have the oldest person in each group lie down in the center of his or her circle and pretend to be dead. If necessary, remind the "dead" group members of the seriousness of the activity and ask them to remain motionless. Say: *The person lying in the center of your circle was killed because of another's disobedience to God. He or she has just been killed by the angel of death. As a corpse, he or she cannot move or participate in the rest of this activity in any way. In your circles, discuss these questions now.*

Allow kids a moment or two to discuss each of the following questions. Starting with the youngest person in each group, have kids take turns reporting their groups' answers after discussing each question.

Ask: *How do you feel standing over a corpse that was killed because someone disobeyed God? Explain. What do you think it might've been like if the firstborn children in ancient Egypt had known they were going to die because of Pharaoh's disobedience? What would your feelings be if you knew the angel of death was coming tonight to kill not just the firstborn, but all who've been disobedient to God? Like it or not, we're all destined to die.*

Death of the Firstborn

What do you think waits for those who've disobeyed God during their lives? Describe it.

RESPONSE

Say: *The story doesn't end with the death of the firstborn. God provided a way of escape for his followers—a lamb sacrificed in their place. This lamb became known as the Passover lamb, because when the angel of death saw its blood on a family's house, the angel "passed over" that house and let the firstborn live.*

Have groups read Revelation 5:9-10. Ask: *What thoughts came into your mind as you read this Scripture? Why do you think it was necessary for Jesus to die for our disobedience? How does it feel knowing that Jesus became the lamb that was sacrificed to provide a way of escape from eternal death for you? Explain. In what ways can Jesus' sacrifice bring you life? How does Jesus' sacrifice affect the way you live each day?*

CLOSING

Have groups say in unison, "Because Jesus died, you can live again!" to their "dead" group members and raise them back to "life."

Then form one large circle of all group members. Have kids hold hands as you pray a prayer like this: *Thank you, Jesus, for being our Passover lamb. We won't forget how you sacrificed your life so we could be saved from eternal death. Help us to live each day in such a way as to make you proud of us. Amen.*

Paper-Airplane Resurrections

- **Theme:** Easter
- **Scripture:** 1 Corinthians 15:12-14
- **Overview:** Kids will discover the importance of Jesus' resurrection.
- **Preparation:** You'll need paper for paper airplanes, an empty box with a lid, a black marker, a bag of small candy bars, and Bibles.

EXPERIENCE

Distribute the paper and say: *Use your paper to create the best airplane you possibly can for a paper-airplane-throwing contest. The winner of this contest will receive a candy bar. When your plane is ready, bring it to me. Our contest will begin in three minutes, so start building your planes now.*

After three minutes collect all the airplanes and say: *We have some pretty sharp looking planes here.* Put all the planes in the box and close the lid. On the outside of the box write "Rest in Peace" with a black marker. Say: *Sorry, the paper-airplane contest has been killed. There is no winner; all the planes have been buried inside this box.*

RESPONSE

Wait for kids' reactions. Then have kids stand as you ask the following questions. Tell group members you'd like to hear lots of interesting answers and allow kids to respond after each question. When one student shares an answer, anyone who thought of the same answer and has nothing more to add may sit down. When all kids are seated, ask the next question and repeat the process.

Ask: *What did you think when your airplanes were "buried" in the box? What good are the airplanes if they stay buried?*

Have someone wearing yellow read 1 Corinthians 15:12-14.
Ask: *How does the burial of our airplanes compare to Jesus'*

Paper-Airplane Resurrections

death and burial? What good would our faith be if Jesus had been buried but never raised from the dead? What are your thoughts about Jesus' resurrection? How does Jesus' resurrection affect your faith? your daily life?

CLOSING

Have kids line up against one wall. Open the box and pass it down the line, allowing kids to "resurrect" their airplanes by removing them from the box.

On the count of three, have everyone shout, "I can fly high because Jesus is alive!" and throw their airplanes. Declare everyone a winner and give everyone a candy-bar prize.

Seeing the Person in the Parent

■ **Theme:** Mother's Day or Father's Day
■ **Scripture:** Galatians 5:14-15
■ **Overview:** Group members will test themselves on how well they know their parents.
■ **Preparation:** You'll need newsprint, a marker, photocopies of the "Parent Interview" handout (p. 104), and Bibles.

EXPERIENCE

Ask kids the following questions about their parents. After each question, have any group members who are confident they know the answer stand up and share it with the group. Remind kids to be honest and not to guess at answers.

Write on newsprint the approximate percentage of the group that stands up after each question. For example, if you have 15 students, and seven kids stand after a question, write "50%."

Ask:
● *What's your mother or father's favorite holiday and why?*
● *What was the name of your mother or father's high school sweetheart?*
● *What was your mother or father's favorite music group in high school?*
● *What's your mother or father's favorite book?*
● *What's one dream your mother or father had when she or he was young?*
● *Why did your mother or father decide to live in this community?*
● *What has been your mother or father's greatest disappointment in life?*
● *What has been your mother or father's greatest achievement?*

Add up the total of the percentages and divide by eight to get an average percentage for all the questions. Ask kids: *Judging on a scale in which 60 percent is a D, 70 percent is a C,*

Seeing the Person in the Parent

80 percent is a B, and 90 percent is an A, what kind of grade do we get for how well we know our parents?

RESPONSE

Form groups of no more than three. Tell groups to assign one person to act as a representative who will report the group's ideas to the the large group, another to act as the Scripture reader, and a third to be an encourager who urges everyone to participate in the discussion.

Have the Scripture reader read Galatians 5:14-15. Then ask groups to discuss the following questions. Write the questions on newsprint so kids can refer back to them during discussions. Ask: *How does our score on this parent test make you feel? Explain. How would you feel if your parents scored like you did on a test checking out how well they know you? How can getting to know parents better help fulfill Galatians 5:14-15 in family life? What makes it hard for you to fulfill Galatians 5:14-15 in regard to your mother or father? How can you show more interest in your mother or father as a person instead of just as a parent?*

End the discussions after three or four minutes and have the representative in each group share responses.

CLOSING

Give everyone a copy of the "Parent Interview" handout (p. 104). Encourage kids to take their handouts home and "interview" their mothers or fathers as a way to see the person in their parents.

Parent Interview

Use the questions below to "interview" your parents as a way to get to know them better.

- What's your favorite holiday and why?

- What was the name of your high school sweetheart?

- What was your favorite music group in high school?

- What's your favorite book?

- What's one dream you had when you were young?

- Why did you decide to live in this community?

- What has been your greatest disappointment in life?

- What has been your greatest achievement?

Here's the Plan

■ **Theme:** Graduation
■ **Scripture:** Jeremiah 29:11
■ **Overview:** Teenagers will compare the planning necessary to win a game to planning life after graduation.
■ **Preparation:** You'll need 3×5 cards, pencils, newsprint, a marker, snacks, and Bibles.

EXPERIENCE

Give each student a 3×5 card and a pencil. List the following items on newsprint: sunscreen, antinausea medicine, umbrella, adhesive bandages, comfortable shoes, money.

Say: *You've planned a day at an amusement park with your friends and can only take three items from this list with you. Write your selections on your card now.*

Next, have everyone stand on one side of the room while you stand on the other. Say: *As I read the following description of your day, take steps according to what you wrote on your card. Anyone who makes it all the way to me will have had the perfect day and will receive a snack reward.*

Read the following aloud:

It's going to be a great day at Loony-Land. You and your friends arrive at the main gates just as they open. Those who brought <u>money</u> for tickets may take three steps forward.

After riding the roller coaster fifteen times in a row everyone's feeling a bit queasy. However, those bringing <u>antinausea medicine</u> are feeling well enough to take two steps forward.

The sun's really beating down on you as you stand in line for the next ride. Those bringing <u>sunscreen</u> or <u>umbrellas</u> are cool enough to wait it out and take two steps forward while everyone else takes a step backward to rest in the shade.

But wait! The sun's being blocked by sudden rain clouds. Those with <u>umbrellas</u> may take two steps forward. Anyone who didn't bring an umbrella has to take a step backward to get under shelter.

Finally the rain stops. You realize you've been walking all day and your feet are killing you. You wonder if you can make it back to the car. If you wore <u>comfortable shoes</u> or brought

Here's the Plan

adhesive bandages for those blisters, take four steps forward. Everyone else must sit down and wait for the bus.

Award a snack prize to anyone who made it to you. If no one made it across the room, determine the guy and girl who are closest to you and award them a snack for planning their day so wisely.

RESPONSE

Have everyone stand in a circle as you ask the next questions. When someone shares a response, have others who thought of the same answer and have nothing more to add take one step backward. After everyone has stepped backward, re-form the circle and repeat the process for all remaining questions.

Ask: _How did you choose what to bring along? How would you have chosen differently now that you know how the game turned out? How is this like planning for life after high school? How can you plan wisely for life after graduation? How were the surprises you faced in this game like the surprises people face even when they plan as well as they can?_

Say: _Graduation is a time for making plans for the future._ Ask: _What feelings do you have about planning for life after graduation?_

Have kids read Jeremiah 29:11 aloud in unison and ask: _How can this verse encourage you as you plan for life after graduation? Why do you think God included this verse in the Bible? How can you discover God's plans for your future?_

Say: _No matter how well you plan for life after high school, circumstances will still catch you unprepared at times. During those times, you can take comfort in the encouragement of Jeremiah 29:11._

CLOSING

Form groups of no more than four. Starting with the oldest person in each foursome, have group members complete this sentence to encourage each other about life after graduation: "I

Here's the Plan

predict you'll be (occupation) because you (positive trait)."

For example, kids might say, "I predict you'll be a dentist because you have such a great smile."

After everyone has been affirmed, have all the seniors in your group stand as you close with a short prayer asking for God's guidance in their future.

Summer Adventures

〰〰〰〰〰〰〰〰〰〰〰〰

- **■ Theme:** Summer vacation
- **■ Scripture:** Galatians 6:1-10
- **■ Overview:** Group members will examine how following the instructions of Galatians 6:1-10 can create a spiritual summer adventure.
- **■ Preparation:** Photocopy and cut apart enough "Summer Adventures" handouts (p. 110) for each group member to have 10 cards. You'll also need Bibles.

EXPERIENCE

Shuffle the "Summer Adventures" cards to thoroughly mix them up. Give each group member 10 cards (it's OK if kids have duplicate cards).

Say: *You've got 60 seconds to get a complete set of all 10 "Summer Adventures" cards—with no duplicates. You may trade one card at a time with anyone else in the group, but never two cards in a row with the same person. Remember, you've only got 60 seconds, so you'll have to hurry. Ready? Go.*

Tell kids to call out cards they have available for trade; for example, "I have one 'Carry your own load' card! Anyone want to trade?" Have kids trade for 60 seconds, or until one has a set of all 10 adventure cards (it's OK if kids don't have complete sets at the end of trading).

Afterward ask kids to respond to these questions: *What's your reaction to what you just did? Explain. What would your summer vacation be like if it reflected your experience during this game? if it reflected the instructions on your cards? In what ways would following the instructions on your cards make your summer vacation a spiritual adventure? What would keep you from acting out the instructions on your cards?*

RESPONSE

Give kids who didn't get all 10 of the "Summer Adventures" cards earlier a minute or two of trading time to complete their sets. Form groups of no more than three. Have the person wearing the brightest colors in each group read Galatians 6:1-10

Summer Adventures

aloud. Then say: *Summer vacation gives an opportunity to begin changes that can bring positive results all year long. In your trios, choose one summer adventure from your cards, and brainstorm three ways you can start that adventure at home this summer.*

Kids might say, "I can help a friend through a difficult time to fulfill Galatians 6:2," "I can help fulfill Galatians 6:6 by volunteering to help out during Sunday school or midweek meetings," or "I can start a home Bible club for kids in my neighborhood to fulfill Galatians 6:7."

CLOSING

Have trios take turns standing in front while you say a short prayer similar to this for each group: *God, thanks for giving us the opportunity to start a spiritual adventure by serving you this summer. Help us turn these summer adventures of service into lifetime adventures of following you. In Jesus' name, amen.*

Encourage the rest of the group to say silent prayers while you pray aloud. Continue until you've prayed for every trio in the group. (If your class is large, you may want to have two or three trios stand up front at the same time.)

Summer Adventures

Photocopy and cut out enough cards for each student to have 10.

Gently help to correct the sins you see (Galatians 6:1).	Help support your Bible teachers (Galatians 6:6).
Help carry each other's burdens (Galatians 6:2).	Think through the results of your actions; choose actions that bring about good (Galatians 6:7).
Don't be conceited (Galatians 6:3).	Notice the harm caused by sin; choose good rather than sin (Galatians 6:8).
Compete only with yourself; don't compare yourself to others (Galatians 6:4).	Keep doing good no matter how hard it gets; it will be worth it (Galatians 6:9).
Carry your own load (Galatians 6:5).	Do good to all people, especially to other Christians (Galatians 6:10).

Set Me Free

- **Theme:** Independence Day
- **Scripture:** 2 Peter 2:18-19; John 8:31-32
- **Overview:** Group members will compare being tied up with thread to the way sin ties people up in life.
- **Preparation:** You'll need a spool of thread for every two group members, scissors, and Bibles.

EXPERIENCE

Say: *Independence Day is our nation's celebration of breaking free from England to form our own country. But even in our own country, Americans still struggle to break free from sin. Let's do an exercise to explore this further.*

Form pairs and give each pair a spool of thread. Have kids number off by twos within their pairs. Next, have all the ones tie one loop of thread around their partners' wrists.

Say: *On the count of three, try to break the thread that binds your wrists. One, two, three!*

After kids have broken the thread, have the twos tie a loop of thread around their partners' wrists. Count to three again and have the ones break the thread.

Ask: *Was anybody worried about breaking free from the thread? Why or why not?*

Say: *Let's try this again, only this time I want the ones to tie 25 loops of thread around the twos' wrists. Go.*

After all twos have their wrists tied up, count to three again and see if anyone can break free (most won't be able to). Then have pairs discuss the following questions while the twos are still tied up. After each question, allow a few moments for discussion, then have one person in each pair share his or her pair's responses with the group.

Ask: *What are your feelings about this activity so far? Explain. How did something as weak as thread gain such power over the twos so easily?*

RESPONSE

Have ones in each pair read aloud 2 Peter 2:18-19. Ask: *In*

Set Me Free

what ways is sin like the thread in this activity? What makes people experiment with sin? How does sin tie us up in life? in our relationships with others? in our relationship with God? How can we break free from the power of sin?

CLOSING

Read aloud John 8:31-32. Then pass around a pair of scissors to the ones in each pair. Have ones take turns saying to their partners, "The truth shall make you free!" as they cut the thread from the twos' wrists.

Close by saying: *Jesus gives a real reason to celebrate Independence Day because he can set us free from sin.*

On the First Day of School

- ■ **Theme:** New school year
- ■ **Scripture:** Philippians 3:13-14
- ■ **Overview:** Group members will discuss their expectations for the new school year.
- ■ **Preparation:** You'll need paper, pencils, and a Bible.

EXPERIENCE

Form a circle and give each student a sheet of paper and a pencil. Have kids write their names at the top of their papers. Then have each person start writing a story beginning with the phrase, "On the first day of school ... "

After 30 seconds, have group members write "and then ... " and pass their papers to the person on their right. Have kids continue writing on the new papers without reading what has already been written. Repeat this process every 15 to 30 seconds until papers have returned to their owners. The results will be a collection of hilarious stories.

RESPONSE

Give everyone a minute to read the finished papers.

Then ask: *What did you expect your finished paper to look like? How did the final product match your expectations? What expectations do you have for the new school year? How do you respond when the school year, like your paper, doesn't turn out the way you expect? What can you do to make your school year turn out better than you expect?*

Have the person who lives closest to the church read Philippians 3:13-14 aloud.

Ask: *How can imitating the attitude of Philippians 3:13-14 help make your school year turn out better than you expect? What keeps you from imitating Paul's attitude in Philippians 3:13-14? How can we help each other follow the advice of this verse during the new school year?*

On the First Day of School

CLOSING

Tell kids to pretend the end of the school year has come. Have kids turn their papers over and write a short yearbook note to themselves. Tell them to describe the things they hope to have accomplished by the end of the year.

For example, kids might write, "Congratulations on getting an A in biology. Also, you were great in the drama presentation this year. I'm looking forward to spending next year with you. Sincerely, Me."

Have kids take home their papers as reminders of their goals for the new school year.

Thankfulness Search

- **Theme:** Thanksgiving
- **Scripture:** Luke 17:11-19
- **Overview:** Group members will search for items they're thankful for and discuss Luke 17:11-19.
- **Preparation:** You'll need paper, pencils, and Bibles.

EXPERIENCE

Form groups of no more than four and give paper and pencils to each group.

Say: *You have four minutes to go around the church grounds and find 20 things your group is thankful for. List these things on your paper and be prepared to explain why your group is thankful for the things on your list. Go.*

Send everyone out to search. Remind kids to search quietly and to not disturb other groups. When the foursomes return, have groups select representatives to report their discoveries and explain why they're thankful for the items they listed. Kids' lists might include things such as friends, nature, a building to worship in, and food.

RESPONSE

Have the person in each group whose favorite pizza topping is pepperoni read aloud Luke 17:11-19. Then have groups discuss these questions, one at a time. After each discussion, have a different representative report his or her group's responses to everyone else.

Ask: *What were you thinking while you made your lists? Explain. How often have you thanked God for the things on your lists? Why is it sometimes easy to neglect thanking God for all he does? Why do you think the nine lepers in Luke 17:11-19 neglected to thank Jesus for healing them? How do you think Jesus felt when the one leper came back to thank him? How can we help one another imitate the attitude of the thankful leper this week? this month? this year?*

Thankfulness Search

CLOSING

Say: *As we can see from our lists, we've got plenty to be thankful for. Let's take time right now to thank God for all he does.*

Have foursomes pass their lists among themselves and take turns saying sentence prayers of thanks for the items they listed. If time allows, continue until all items have been read from all the lists.

The Best Gift Ever

- **Theme:** Christmas
- **Scripture:** Luke 2:8-11
- **Overview:** Group members will examine how God's Son was "the best gift ever."
- **Preparation:** You'll need a Bible.

EXPERIENCE

Form pairs and have each pair choose an item in the room to defend as the "greatest gift anyone could ever receive." The items don't have to be fancy; they can be as simple as a paper clip or an eraser. But pairs must be ready to defend theirs as the best gift ever.

After everyone has chosen their gifts, form a circle and have pairs take turns explaining why theirs is the best gift. After all groups have shared, have kids vote on which gift in the circle truly is the "greatest gift ever."

RESPONSE

Read Luke 2:8-11 aloud. Have pairs discuss the following questions and report their answers to the group.

Ask: *What were your thoughts during this activity? Explain. How did hearing the story of Jesus' birth make you feel about the "greatest gifts ever" we discussed earlier? Explain. What kind of defense can you make for the statement, "Jesus is the greatest gift ever"? How does the gift of Jesus 2,000 years ago affect your life today? What's difficult about receiving the gift of Jesus? How can we receive the gift of Jesus today?*

CLOSING

Say: *The best Christmas gift ever was the first one given— Jesus Christ. Let's sing a song to honor and thank Jesus for that gift of himself.*

To close have kids hold hands while they sing a Christmas carol such as "Away in a Manger" or "Silent Night! Holy Night!"

Build Faith in Your Teenagers With...

DEVOTIONS FOR YOUTH GROUPS

Get 52 quick devotions in each book that need little or no preparation—on important topics such as...

- love,
- friendship,
- rumors,
- peer pressure,
- faith,
- accepting others,
- grades,
- peace,
- service,

...and more. Each is complete with Scripture reference, attention-grabbing learning experience, discussion questions, and closing. Bring teenagers closer to God with these refreshing devotions!

10-Minute Devotions for Youth Groups
J.B. Collingsworth
ISBN 0-931529-85-9

More 10-Minute Devotions for Youth Groups
ISBN 1-55945-068-1

DEVOTIONS FOR YOUTH GROUPS ON THE GO

Dan and Cindy Hansen

Now it's easy to turn every youth group trip into an opportunity for spiritual growth for your kids. This resource gives you 52 easy-to-prepare devotions that teach meaningful spiritual lessons using the experiences of your group's favorite outings. You'll get devotions perfect for everything from amusement parks, to choir trips, to miniature golf, to the zoo. Your kids will gain new insights from the Bible as they...

- discuss how many "strikes" God gives us—after enjoying a game of softball,
- experience the hardship of Jesus' temptation in the wilderness—on a camping trip,
- understand the disciples' relief when Jesus calmed the storm—while white-water rafting, even

...learn to trust God's will when bad weather cancels an event or the bus breaks down!

Plus, the handy topical listing makes your planning easy.

ISBN 1-55945-075-4

YOUTH GROUP TRUST BUILDERS

Denny Rydberg

Positive peer pressure can result when teenagers have close, supportive relationships with other teenagers who share the same faith. Helping to build this caring community is the goal of this valuable new resource from youth ministry veteran Denny Rydberg. You'll discover a unique five-step approach to building a sense of community in youth groups...
- Bond Building—creating an environment of trust,
- Opening Up—encouraging open sharing and listening,
- Affirming—giving sincere compliments,
- Stretching—conquering obstacles, and
- Deeper Sharing and Goal Setting—increasing accountability.

With each step is a series of interactive exercises to help teenagers grow in these important areas. Perfect for youth ministry meetings from the church classroom to wilderness camping, these exercises are easy to prepare and need only simple supplies.

ISBN 1-55945-172-6

101 AFFIRMATIONS FOR TEENAGERS

Encourage your kids to love themselves and others. Use this value-filled resource to help your teenagers...
- feel good about themselves,
- build confidence in their abilities,
- handle their emotional ups and downs,
- learn to love and accept others, and
- appreciate Jesus' model of unconditional love.

Each chapter provides down-to-earth affirmations for adding new dimension to your ministry. You'll be encouraged as...
- your young people are excited about being part of the group,
- newcomers can't wait to return for the next meeting,
- the tough kids open up,
- cliques and quarrels vanish, and
- those who are hurting heal.

Use these ready-in-a-flash affirmations to bring kids together—and build nurturing relationships that lead them closer to God.

ISBN 1-55945-176-9

Bible-Based Programming Ideas...

THE 13 MOST IMPORTANT BIBLE LESSONS FOR TEENAGERS

Build a strong foundation of basic Bible understanding with these active lessons that make learning fun. You'll get 13 complete programs on topics like...
- Who is Jesus?
- What is the Bible?
- Why does life hurt?
- Why the church?

...plus, you'll teach lessons on prayer, witnessing, practical service, and end times. Perfect to help new Christians understand their faith or to refresh mature believers. The 13-week format works well for Sunday school or youth meetings.

ISBN 1-55945-261-7

LIFE-CHANGING BIBLE STUDIES FROM THE NEW TESTAMENT

Teach your teenagers about the New Testament while equipping them to live by God's Word each day. The 30 active studies in this book will help your kids see the relevance of key New Testament topics like...
- discipleship,
- faith,
- service,
- Jesus' death and resurrection, and
- Christian living.

You'll make it easy to teach your teenagers—with quick and easy studies that...
- grab kids' attention,
- involve teenagers in the learning process,
- help kids discover Bible truths for themselves, and
- make learning fun.

Use **Life-Changing Bible Studies From the New Testament** to give your kids fun Bible-based sessions that actually make a difference in their lives.

ISBN 1-55945-079-7